LIVE

THE ULTIMATE GUIDE TO

WISER

ADULTING POST-GRAD

PUBLISHING

Baton Rouge, LA

Copyright © 2021 Erin R. Wheeler, PhD
All rights reserved. No part of this book may be reproduced in any form or by any electronic or mechanical means, including information storage and retrieval systems, without permission in writing from the publisher, except by reviewers, who may quote brief passages in a review.

Cover Design: Erin R. Wheeler

ISBN – 9780578816050
EISBN – 9781087861654

Printed and bound in USA

Website: www.erinrwheelerphd.com
Facebook: @erinwheelerphd
Instagram: @erinwheelerphd

For speaking engagements and booking, email: erin.wheeler.00@gmail.com

LIVE

THE ULTIMATE GUIDE TO

WISER

ADULTING POST-GRAD

Dr. Erin Wheeler

TABLE OF CONTENTS

INTRODUCTION 1

POST-GRAD BLUES 7

MY POST-GRAD BLUES 15

RE-CALIBRATE YOUR EXPECTATIONS 23

THE GROWN-UP GLOW UP 43

FLOW AND GO 85

TO LIVE OR TO EXIST? 125

CONFIDENTIAL CAREER COMMANDMENTS 163

MAKING SENSE OF THE DOLLARS 219

LIVE WISER 243

INTRODUCTION

Live Wiser

INTRODUCTION

In 2017, I was let go from my first "big girl" job. It was one of the greatest lessons in adulting ever. I thought I had reached a point that I had dreamed of since I entered college. The good life, you know? I was confused. Not confused that I had been let go from a job where I performed really well, but I was confused that I was more relieved than scared. You see, I was finally getting a break from working and hustling day in and day out. Since 2003, I've always had two, and sometimes, three, jobs. I still worked multiple jobs even after I received my undergraduate degree. Fourteen years later, I was tired. I was sad. I was unsatisfied. Nothing was going according to plan. I was supposed to get my doctorate, begin a tenured track teaching position in biology, and use my summers to host camps for high school students.

That was the plan. Instead, I found myself hovering adjacently close to everything I wanted though it was always out of my grasp. I applied endlessly to jobs everywhere in America. Frustrated, I went into autopilot. I began to just accept the opportunities in front of me and did them with excellence. Being on autopilot actually led me down a path I was not expecting.

It was a good path.

It led me to my pot-of-gold at the end of the college degree rainbow: six-figure salary and a respectable title. It was that "good" job that was promised to us as we applied to, entered, and graduated from college. It took me about eight years to reach that point. However, once I received it and lost it, I began to question everything that was taught to us through the years about life, career, and education. During my time of exploring and consulting (Read: Unemployment), I found myself writing my first book, *Geaux Wiser: Secrets to College Success* to help high school and college students prepare for and complete college. The book was intended to help ease students into a smooth transition from high school to college and to set them up for success after college. It was all about making sure undergraduate students maximize their degree so they can have a successful post-grad life.

Live Wiser mitigates the sting and shock of adulting post-grad. It is full of lessons that high students are not quite ready to hear just yet. Just like *Geaux Wiser*, this book is filled with things I learned too late and learned the hard way. If you look at a bunch of 30-something college graduates and you think they have it all together, you thought wrong. We are just getting it together. We are just finding out our true passions and are being less apologetic about being happy and fulfilled. I speak for my fellow Millennials and Generation X'ers, in saying that adulting is no joke. There are so many things that we would have done differently if someone would have warned us.

Live Wiser is the guide that we wished we would have had to lessen the post-grad blues and prepare accordingly for adulting.

I hope this book inspires you to make the best of your post-college transition no matter where you are on the journey.

Live Wiser

POST-GRAD BLUES

Live Wiser

POST-GRAD BLUES

You may be feeling it now. You may be reading this and have yet to experience it. You may be reading this and will get an epiphany that you've dealt with it. The "IT" that I am referring to is the post-grad blues. I am starting this guide here because this is one of the first stops on the adulting train that no one tells you about. It feels lonely, cold, and sad. Yet, millions of Millennials and Generation X'ers have experienced this same low place in life. I think it was worst for us because we were the first to live our life on social media. We were posting the best of our lives, whether it was totally true or not. I mean who was brave to enough to post a picture of the hundreds of applications you've applied for, or the after-work selfie that showed bags under your eyes, or the status update that details how you are dragging @ss to work at a job you don't really like every morning. No, we posted the pictures of brunch we were barely able to pay for and wrote statuses that alluded to our faux relationships or uploaded the wedding pictures from marriages that lasted just a little longer than the reception. When you see everyone living a golden life and you aren't, you feel like something is wrong with you.

But, most of us were living a lie!

So, there was no reason for us to feel this isolated and lonely in our situation. If you could go behind the posts, pictures, and the statuses to hear our real intimate conversations, you would be truly shocked. That was in 2008 with only Facebook. I can only imagine how that feels for you with so many media outlets. Hell, it's hard for me 12 years removed from college to see my peers flaunt businesses, vacations and hustles while I'm still bootstrapping. Faking it for social media is at an all-time high. The point is that all the glitz and glamour you see on your social media feeds is an illusion. Comparing real-life to illusions will set you up for disappointment every single time. And most of our post-grad blues come from equivalent social comparison. The other contributing factor is outdated social expectations (more on this in Chapter 4).

Dr. Erin Wheeler

I want to normalize the emotions and challenges you feel and experience after college so you can minimize the time you spend soaking and sulking in your post-grad blues. My intent for this chapter was to present you with heavy, thought-provoking research. Womp! Womp! To my surprise there was not a lot of research dedicated to this topic, which feeds into this notion that no one wants to talk about the dark period you experience after the elation of college graduation. However, there are some articles on reputable sites and first-person accounts on blogs. You may also find the term "post-graduation depression" used in many places. According to a CNBC article, it is loosely defined as, "— the condition is characterized by a period of severe sadness, loss of motivation, helplessness and isolation due to constant change and an overabundance of choices." I would amend that definition a little to read: the condition is characterized by a period of severe sadness, loss of motivation, helplessness, and isolation due to constant change, **an increase in rejection and overabundance of decisions.** While this is not an official clinical diagnosis, post-grad blues or depression is a real thing.

So, what are the characteristics of post-grad blues? According to Talkspace (talkspace.com), symptoms include long periods of sadness and the inability to enjoy significant areas of your life like friends and family. There's also the turning heavily to drugs, alcohol to cope with or mask feelings. In comparison, the clinical definition of generalized depression "is a mood disorder that causes a persistent feeling of sadness and loss of interest. Also called major depressive disorder or clinical depression, it affects how you feel, think and behave and can lead to a variety of emotional and physical problems." There are several categories of depression, each differentiated by cause and severity. What is called post-grad blues could encroach on clinical depression. Only a very thin line separates the two. With more focus and research on the topic, I contend that post-grad depression could be and should be included in the official diagnosis.

The second purpose of this chapter is to call attention to mental health. Just because blues sound less serious than depression, doesn't mean that you should shrug it off. They are both connected to your mental health. Getting a therapist was just becoming in vogue during my post-grad years. I probably should have talked with a professional (I kind of did, but not really. More about that in the next chapter). No one encouraged me to take advantage on the resource, which is why I am encouraging you to consider it. With the spotlight on mental health these days, there is little excuse for you to disregard the idea of seeing a professional regardless if you think your symptoms lack severity. Yes, many college graduates experience this, but it is not mandatory that you have suffer through it and start this new chapter in your life with hopelessness.

Live Wiser walks you through each of the areas of your life that could give you grief and provides a new perspective to brighten your outlook to get you out of your post-grad funk or avoid it altogether. But first a deeper look into my post-grad blues.

Live Wiser

MY POST-GRAD BLUES

Live Wiser

MY POST-GRAD BLUES

Before we talk about my post-grad blues, let's rewind to my pre-grad time. I entered Southeastern Louisiana University as a biology major in 2003. I had the fullest intent to make moves as a young, black biomedical scientist as well as to live life to the fullest as a newly liberated college student. To say I had a blast as an undergrad would be an understatement. I was an introvert and a social butterfly. I was in a sorority, student government, and the campus activities board. I worked as a tutor and an admission ambassador. I was elected to the homecoming court. I had great friends with whom I share awesome memories. Friends who became my family. This nerdy, cool, shy girl had found her stride as a young adult. However, after Katrina in 2005 and after a rough junior year, I had had my fill of college.

My senior year was like most students'. It was 2007. I had senioritis. I was anxious and over school.

I was already frustrated that I didn't graduate on time. My GPA was a 2.8 from failing Organic Chemistry 1 and 2 twice and barely passing Physics. This meant I couldn't get into a competitive biology PhD program which wanted at 3.0 or higher. Side Note: it was trending at the time in STEM to skip the Master's and go straight to a PhD to save time and money. I wasn't excited to become a traditional benchtop scientist, but I was excited at the possibility of becoming a faculty member and teaching 1st-year biology. Luckily, a mentor introduced me to a graduate program in Science Education at Southern University Baton Rouge (SUBR). I was really excited for this opportunity.

I graduated in the fall of 2007, so I had about seven months before I began graduate school in the fall of 2008. I worked for six months at an interesting temporary position. I worked 7 days on and 7 days off with 12-hour shifts in a hospital lab. Those seven months were great. I made great money. Vacationed regularly.

Ahh...the good life.

I prepared to move to Baton Rouge in an apartment with my best friend from undergrad. A lot of my college clique and sorority sisters lived in Baton Rouge, so it was a continuation of our undergrad shenanigans. Graduate school wasn't a financial issue for me. I received a full fellowship which helped me to just focus on school and be a professional student. My immediate transition to grad school delayed my post- grad blues. My friends' blues, however, were dark blue and in high gear. Some were dealing the early years of motherhood and marriage, while others were dealing with infertility or failed long-term relationships. A few were battling with career confusion and rejection. We were all dealing with a stank local and national economy (we were of ripe age to deal with the double dip recession) which meant a terrible job market and lack of money.

My blues kicked in shortly after graduating with my PhD. I was 25ish. I had just purchased my home. I was still working in my first full-time adult job. Still, I was not happy at all. My relationship was fizzling out. Of course, I thought I was going to get married. Why? Because he was great, I had graduated, and I was 25. Isn't that what you are supposed to do? I thought that as soon as I finished my PhD that I would have these amazing job offers to teach and move away to some interesting place. I applied to what felt like 100 positions and only received one interview. I had a love-hate relationship with my job. I love the work. I hated the pay. I loved that it was a job that paid. I hated the suffocation I felt working 8:00 AM - 4:30 PM with no flexibility. I loved my co-workers and my boss. I hated wasting 10 hours a week in traffic when my home was 20 minutes away. Hated the lack of opportunity to grow and move up. My financial goals were null and void. I wasn't saving as much as I wanted. Student loans had kicked in. I started tutoring and coaching on the side to make a little extra money. I even worked a second job on the weekend as an Upward Bound instructor. By Sunday afternoon, I was near tears and exhausted. I was worn out from the rat race of the week and the extra side hustles that still didn't get me out of debt and from the feeling of not accomplishing anything in life that made me happy.

I felt trapped.

Trapped by debt, a dead-end career, not knowing who I was, or how to balance my life or even knowing what to do with my life. I felt like a failure. It seemed like I had everything, but I was so empty. All I had was a house that was sucking up my finances and degrees that didn't land me any jobs. I wasn't really dating, wasn't close to marriage, and definitely not in place for kids. At my lowest, I was about 28 or 29, the big 30 was on peering angrily around the corner. I had to do something.

Thank God for my best friend who was a professional counselor. She observed and identified some behaviors associated with functional depression. During one of our Sunday brunches, (Can you ever be too broke for brunch?) we discussed my continued funk. She asked me what my priorities were. She actually used the crayons that came with the kid's menu to draw out the wellness wheel. I used the wellness wheel strategy before with academic coaching students, but I never stopped to use it on myself. So, we talked about my priorities, goals, and what would make me happy. That conversation was a major game changer for my mindset, but not for my situation. I put my priorities in place. What didn't make the top list didn't get my time, energy, or money. I began to become even more frugal. I decided to rethink alternative career paths and put more energy into my start-up so that I can have a creative release and an exit plan from my job. I put the endless unfruitful job search on pause. I even began the work to start a non-profit. Just as I was trying to accessorize and style my shade of post-grad blues to make it work, I received the call.

You know, the call that changes everything.

I was recruited to be an assistant vice president of a university just a month shy of my 30th birthday. I'm now 35. My post-grad season is over. Now, I think my blues are from good old fashioned adulting, the millennial version.

Although my 30s have been a rollercoaster, I don't think I would like to relive my 20s. I am wiser and stronger. I learned an awful lot looking back. My most impactful adulting epiphany centered around expectations. Your first step in conquering adulting post-grad is managing expectations.

RE-CALIBRATE YOUR EXPECTATIONS

RE-CALIBRATE YOUR EXPECTATIONS

Since kindergarten, students are constantly asked what they want to be when they grow up. There's a handful of common and predictable answers: A doctor. An astronaut. A nurse. A lawyer. A famous basketball player. An accountant turned famous YouTube chef. No? No one in your elementary class wanted this? This person would not be the ideal person to receive an invitation to a high school career day. No one dreams of becoming something only to half enjoy it and then switch to something else entirely. We've always been taught that life is linear if you make the right choices and do the right thing. Like, make good grades in school, or pick a "good" career. Go to college. Choose the appropriate major. Graduate. Get a good job. Date. Marry the right person. Stay on a job for a long time. Get promoted. Retire. Live happily ever after.

Live Wiser

I once subscribed to this notion. I thought that I was supposed to be married by 25. I thought I would fall absolutely in love with my first professional job and work my way up and make good money while doing so. None of this happened. Now honestly, I don't know whose plan it was. I think it was all mine. But, I think it was more or so everyone else's plan. Regardless, whose plan it was, it fell apart. Failing a test is one thing. Failing at life is another. I began to feel sorry for myself. Then I realized that my friends with whom I graduated college felt the same way. We each had a piece of the good life. No one had it all. No one was genuinely happy. There were those who had the love and family thing while wishing for a better job. There were those with good jobs who were one step away from quitting. Some were in grad school wishing for an end to the comprehensive examinations or dissertation. We were all new college grads who were miserable because our golden ticket to the good life we were promised was revoked. We continued to push through post-grad years making the best of it. Some kept the status quo and became content with what they had, and others took risks to find their happy place.

Dr. Erin Wheeler

As a 30-something now, 10-15 years removed from college, I've learned quite a few things. The one lesson I wished I knew early on was to expect the unexpected. Formal education prepares us for the expected. It leaves young adults out to dry when life doesn't go as planned. I admired a lot of professional, successful people. I saw the great job, the nice car, the home, the marriage, the family. Yet, seeing is different than knowing what they went through. During the Pity Tour of my 20s as I sadly questioned and sought answers, I spoke with a lot of people to figure out what I was doing wrong. The answers were bittersweet.

Many of the successful professionals I encounter fell into opportunities. Some worked in jobs closely related to their degree. Most stumble their way into what they have. Almost all hated their first job. A minority group was still working with the same employer who hired them right out of college. Plenty were still searching for purpose, identifying their true passion, and longing to achieve a long list of dreams that had been deferred since their youth. Some were happily single and never married. Some were happily divorced and ready to mingle. Everyone had a unique story or path that had me wanting to hear more. There were stories of pain, sadness, joy, redemption.

I, then, realized that everyone has their own personal journey. My mindset and perspective about life shifted. I reassessed the value of college. I changed my expectations of career and finances. I drastically changed my definition of success. And, most importantly, I re-calibrated my barometer for happiness.

About a week before I began writing this chapter, I listened to my pastor's sermon entitled, "Make Yourself Happy". The main point of which was that you should set the criteria for happiness. By extension, I believe, you also set the criteria for success. Hence, the purpose of this chapter is to encourage you to hit the reset button on your thoughts and beliefs about success and happiness, the two things that are unconsciously tied to a college education, career and wealth. I want you not only to hit the reset button, but to also re-calibrate your own expectations and redefine what success and happiness means to you. Once I re-calibrated my expectations in life, defined my own happiness my post-grad blues began to diminish. My gratitude list became longer, and I was no longer tired from living someone else's life. I encourage you to re-think your expectations of various aspects of life.

While your expectations must be your own, here's my perspective on a few things:

Value of a College Degree

There's a lot of debate on the value of a college degree. Some experts say that earning a college degree it is critical to improve the quality of life. Others say just a high school diploma and some type of higher education is needed. Regardless of rhetoric, it is common thought that a college degree will lead to great things. At our high school graduation, we heard that a college degree will change our lives and provide us with the life we've dreamed of. At college graduation, we heard that our degree will help us change the world. All speeches make it seem that the day after commencement all graduates will be curing cancer and brokering world peace. A few months after we graduate, our families think that we should have a job secured, pay all of our own bills, buy a house, and a new car. Those expectations are not grounded in reality.

Even with three degrees, none of that is guaranteed. It's just the world we live in. It's just life. Here's what I believe. The totality of college is what should be valued, not just the degree. You should not expect a degree to automatically get you a job and a stellar pay. College is a training ground for the real world. While it may not teach you 100% of what you need to know, it prepares you to learn anything. It helps extend your network, broadens your cultural awareness, increases your exposure to new things, and provides a safe space to test new beliefs and values.

College provides you with opportunities to hone your leadership, collaborative, and communication skills that are valued by employers. These are the things that separate a non-graduate from a grad. That's what college is for. That's the value. College is just one piece of the success puzzle. It represents a significant piece of the puzzle if you maximize your college experience, but it's still just a piece. There's still more work to do after you graduate. There's more to learn, more people to meet, more growing, and more discovering to do. All this means is that you shouldn't become discouraged if you can't find the perfect job that aligns with your major or if the first step on your career path is not what you expected. Don't automatically assume that our degree is worthless if your college didn't prepare you for 100% of problems you encounter in the real world. Let your degree serve its foundational purpose and intentionally set out to accessorize (or overhaul) it and fill in any gaps on your own.

Or you can sit and whine about it and remain stagnant.

Because you are reading this you are not going to do the latter. So, how do you accessorize your degree? Well, that leads me to my next point. Re-calibrate your expectations about jobs and career.

Jobs and Career

I had no concept of career as it is loosely defined. Most successful people I know retired from the same profession if not the same job. While I was uneasy at the thought of staying at one place and doing the same thing for 30 years, I thought this was the norm and I set my expectations accordingly. I think it all became clear to me that I needed to re-calibrate my expectations during a time when I became disenchanted with both my job and career at the same time. It was a miserable place to be. This didn't happen immediately after college graduation. I was 10 years post-grad. I felt as if I was too old and too young to start down another path. Being let go of my job because of budget cuts worsened my confusion.

A series of experiences both before and after my job transition taught me so much about careers. There were two experiences that were most significant. The first was a two-week leadership retreat for women in higher education hosted by HERS (Higher Education Resource Services). There, I was immersed in prime career advice and surrounded by accomplished women in executive leadership positions. I listened attentively to their stories. All were different, which was refreshing. Some always planned to be a college president; others drifted into it. Yet, a single thread connected them all: no one's story was linear. They used past experiences to get their next job to gain more experience for their next job, and many jobs were from different fields.

Later that year, I attended a women's retreat in which I met ladies in their 60s who wanted to rebrand and change careers. My encounter with these ladies reaffirmed what I learned that summer. In fact, the creator of the retreat, I later realized, was preparing for her next phase after she retired from a prominent position in which she made history. I met an African American Wall-Street Executive who trades by day and sings opera by night and found time to write a book in her spare time. While these examples of phases and evolution spoke to me, there are many in popular culture today.

Think about the greats. Being President may be thought of as an ultimate job, but President Obama didn't just go back home and do nothing (although he could have). He went on to build his foundation, write books, and even produce films for Netflix. LeBron, although still playing basketball, is gearing up for life after basketball. He's eyeing jobs in Hollywood. He's been producing movies for the last five years. While he did not attend college, he is making sure students in his hometown have an opportunity to go for free as well have access to a quality secondary education with his new school. The takeaway: be flexible, open, and prepared for new opportunities. I realized there really isn't an ultimate job. There may be significant ones, but if you are continually evolving, there will never be an ultimate job.

We are living longer and accomplishing our biggest dreams faster and earlier. Technology and innovation are causing career fields and jobs to be created and phased out at a rapid pace. Everyone who is 50 or younger must be prepared to evolve just as quickly. Education and industry are connected; however, higher education doesn't adapt as quickly as industry. This means that the shelf life of both our college degree and our career path is relatively short. Young professionals will find themselves re-inventing themselves every 7-10 years. The chances of Generation X and Millennials retiring from the same employer in the same field or industry are slim.

So, what should my perspective be regarding career?

First adopt a new definition. *Oxford* defines "career" as, "an occupation undertaken for a significant period of a person's life and with opportunities to progress." That's a pretty good definition. However, *Cambridge* offers another that I like in particular: "the job or series of jobs that you do during your working life, especially when this involves making progress to better jobs or is in a particular profession." I like the series part. When I see "series", I think about order, strategy, progression, and intentionality. The series element was missing from my original perspective of "career". When I adopted the Cambridge version, I began to take control of my career and strategize my series of jobs and determine what qualifies as a "better" job.

The "series of jobs" version keeps in line with the times as jobs become quickly outdated. This definition helps to retrain your brain to think that a career doesn't mean longevity at one job or in one field. This means that if your first job doesn't go well, you don't have to automatically feel like a failure. You can have the confidence to go into the job market and expect to evolve every few years. Thinking in this way will prevent complacency and stagnation. Knowing that you will always need to learn and master new things will always fuel your thirst for knowledge and curiosity. In this way, single jobs take on a new value. You should look at a job as a means to earn money, grow professionally, gain new skills, showcase past knowledge, and meet new people so that you can progress to another position where you level up with the same objectives of making more money, gaining more skills, and network with more people.

Now let me make one thing clear: there is a thin line between being an uncommitted and unfocused job hopper and strategically moving from one job to another. I'm advocating for the latter, of course. To prevent carelessly job hopping, you should develop a strategic plan for your career. I suggest taking the backwards approach. My first book speaks to new college students about doing a time jump into at least 15 years into the future and envisioning their ideal position and salary. Not just dream about it but search for positions that you wouldn't be qualified for now but would be with some time and experience. After researching, I encouraged readers to walk backwards in time to the present and select jobs that would move them strategically to their ideal position. I chose to include this content in the book for undergraduates hoping they wouldn't make the same mistakes I made of inadequate planning. Also, I hoped they would take advantage of their time in college and gain as much experience as possible to prevent going into the job search without an advantage. Although you have graduated, it's not too late to apply the backwards career planning approach.

Money

You can't talk about career without talking about money. One of the main reasons we pursued a degree was to make more money. As you inch closer to college graduation and begin to shed the poor college student life, you could taste the life that comes with a full-time job. You imagine having enough money to swag out an apartment, to drive a nice car, and to take a few Instagram-worthy trips. You may even think that most of your problems will go away with a full-time job with benefits. I would caution you to rethink your perspective of money and the cost of living as a full adult. As an adult, your basic needs expand as your understanding of wealth grows and your priorities shift. I am going to assume that you want to be wealthy, as you didn't graduate college just to live paycheck to paycheck. I'm intentionally using the word "wealthy" instead of rich since being rich can be temporal but being wealthy has more permanence. Building wealth takes time. Don't let Instagram trick you into thinking that you can flip a few houses or build a few businesses overnight and be set for life. It takes real strategies, sacrifice, and years of consistency to build wealth and even more importantly, generational wealth. So, in fine-tuning your perspective of money, you have to think conservatively, strategically, and with foresight. So just be prepared to find that you can't ball on $30k per year (responsibly). The chapter on money will hopefully give you a preview of all the scary parts of the financial side of adulting.

Dating, Marriage and Family

(Girl's name) and *(boy's name)* sitting in the tree
K-i-s-s-i-n-g! *(spell it out)*
First comes love.
Then comes marriage.
Then comes baby* in the baby carriage

I know society sells this part of the American Dream package. Don't get me wrong. All of this is great. Part of adjusting your thinking on this issue is all about timing and pace. There is no deadline for getting married and having kids. There are no rules for getting married in your 20's or after you have completed college. Many post-grads feel rushed into marriage and family or frustrated when there's not even an option for consideration. When society makes this a requirement for a happy life, we feel empty when it doesn't happen in time or how we pictured it in our mind. This can play a huge part in post-grad blues. But, it doesn't have to. Throw out society's expectations and adopt your own. Don't put an age or a year to your expectations. Instead, set an intention to be the person you want to marry. I'm almost certain that you want a partner who is self-aware, self-assured, driven, accomplished, stable (emotionally, mentally, and financially). Be intentional about achieving these qualities for yourself first before you attempt to create a life with someone else. Trust that somewhere on your journey to healing and self-actualization, you will find a person who is willing to meet you where you are and grow with you. Get comfortable with the idea of being single. Recalibrating your standards for starting a family, helps you to enjoy every season of your life, trust timing, focus inward and grow.

Success

Lastly, re-calibrate your definition of success. While social comparison has been around for ages, the age of social media has placed social comparison on steroids. We get bombarded everyday with images of success: luxury clothes, homes, cars, vacations. Everybody is winning. Or are they? Rarely will someone share their failures. So much so that when we fail, we feel like we are the only one. When we feel lonely in the pit of failure, we become stagnant and disappointed. Stagnation means no action, and inaction leads to 100% chance of not succeeding.

I challenge you as you embark on your own path-- stay focused and in your lane. Don't look to your left and right to see what everybody else is doing. Don't compare yourself to your peers. Your journey is unique and so are your criteria for success. I challenge you to set your own parameters for success and stand confidently in your decision. I also challenge you to change your relationship with failure. Failure happens to everyone all the time. It's going to happen to you. It's nearly guaranteed when you try to do big things. It's a part of life. You can let failure, or the fear of failure, inhibit your dreams, or you can leverage it to catapult you closer to success. Smart planning can help you lessen the risk of failure. However, in the event of failure, you should take every opportunity to learn why it happened and adjust your plan to prevent mistakes in the future. If you never learn from your mistakes or unsuccessful situations, your life will be like a bad movie on repeat.

Expectations frame our lives. They provide depth and clarity in our decision making. They help us to measure our progress and grade our choices. Expectations control our emotions and determine our happiness. Shifting your perspective of the world and readjusting your expectations is critical in lessening post-grad blues and surviving adulthood.

Live Wiser

THE GROWN-UP GLOW UP

Live Wiser

THE GROWN-UP GLOW UP
(The GUGU)

Can you remember the first Christmas break after your first semester in college? You remember the confidence you had? The "I'm a little grown" swag? Something happens between the summer after high school graduation and the first semester of college that changes the air you have about you. You feel different about yourself. Everyone can see it.

We have several glow up moments in life. High school to college is one. Kindergarten to 1st grade is another. However, the best glow up is the Grown-Up Glow Up (GUGU). This doesn't come with age, as there are a lot of dull and immature adults. The GUGU only comes with intentional work.

What are the characteristics of individuals who have achieved the GUGU?

- They are unbothered by life's trials and challenges and see them as an opportunity to fight, win and grow.

- They are unapologetically living in their purpose. They are willing to make sacrifices to be fulfilled by their reason for being.

- They are grateful for every little thing in life, good or bad.

- While they have times of fleeting sadness, they have unconditional joy which is based on their consistent statement of gratefulness.

- They understand themselves through and through all the while continuing to make self-discoveries every day. They acknowledge their strengths, accept their flaws, and strive to be a better version of themselves constantly.

- They know how to regulate their emotional health. Although they may deal with anxiety, depression, or other mental illnesses, they know how to control their environment, secure help, and do the work to sustain mental and emotional wellness.

So how do you gain the GUGU? You must become intentionally self-aware, gain emotional stability, and find your purpose in life. Let's look at each step.

Mirror, Mirror: Harnessing the Power of Self-Awareness

Self-awareness is a powerful skill. Most of us think we are really aware of ourselves, but we are *really* disillusioned at times. We hide and disavow our flaws and weaknesses out of shame and embarrassment. We puff up our strengths out of pride and a natural need to compete. My doctoral dissertation centered on first-year college students judging their own ability to study college biology and their confidence in passing the course. Most students said, overwhelmingly so, that their study strategies are top notch, and that they will pass the course with flying colors. When I asked, specifically, how they studied, they just said they read and reviewed the notes. Nothing astounding. However, most of the students failed their first test horribly. However, they stuck by their actions and study habits as being solid. They choose to place the blame on the test and the circumstances. When I had opportunities to speak with students individually throughout the semester, I asked them to reflect and document everything they did during test prep. They were surprised to learn that they had not really been truthful with themselves in that they didn't study as long as and as often as they thought and the strategies that they used were not the best. Once the mirror is present and they really looked at themselves with intent to discover, they had an "ah, ha" moment that provided an opportunity for change and improvement. Being truly self-aware is a continued journey and not an instant one-off activity. Self-evaluation is the beginning of the journey.

Self-evaluation is a really hard thing to do. We fear it sometimes because we are afraid of the "bad things" we'll find out. However, being afraid of learning about our flaws will always lead to us being ignorant of our strengths. Both the strengths and weaknesses add volume to our story. You have to be ready to accept everything you discover about yourself. Sometimes it is not always about turning into a different person but mostly being able to adapt to different situations while leveraging both your redeemable qualities and your flaws to your advantage. The same person who is seen as persistent and courageous can be labeled as stubborn and overly confident depending on the circumstances.

That person is me.

The reason that I was able to have a perfect GPA in high school is also the same reason I failed Organic Chemistry 1 & 2--twice. Yep, you read that correctly. I kept saying I can pass this class even when I failed the first two tests and I saw how many of my peers withdrew before they received an F on their transcript. I'll give you the adulting example: I probably should have sold my home after it was flooded, instead I kept it and struggled to remodel while paying the mortgage. My persistence or stubbornness blinded me to reality and deafened me to sound advice. I suffered greater consequences because I regarded exiting the situation and giving up as failure. I talked myself into keeping the flooded out, gutted out house when I saw lots of for sale signs in my neighborhood. In both instances, I kept saying I'm not a quitter, I am smart, and I can figure this out. But, the wiser action was to retreat, withdraw, and re-strategize to avoid long-term consequences. When I realized that some of my most devastating times were caused by my greatest strength of persistence, it hurt. I thought it was a hard lesson. I now know how to balance, adapt, and check myself when it comes to sticking with something or abandoning it. Self-assessment is hard, but the resulting information is invaluable. Being self-aware puts you in control of your own life. It allows you to define yourself first before your environment does.

Mastering others is strength. Mastering yourself is power. Knowing others is wisdom. Knowing yourself is enlightenment. - Lao Tzu

Conducting a self-evaluation is continuous practice. It starts simply by asking yourself questions. "How or what" questions provide greater depth than "why" questions. How usually entails steps and actions. Steps and actions can be modified. Why involves reason, which is less actionable. Begin with questioning everyday occurrences. For instance, ask yourself, "how do I end up 30 minutes late for work every day?" or "what causes my anxiety to increase?" You build up to a critical analysis of your thoughts, your feelings, and your behaviors daily. Make connections with your failures, your successes, your happiness, and your progress. Don't just think about yourself in isolation. Reflect on how your thoughts, feelings, and behavior affect other people and how they see you. Journaling is a way to capture these questions and answers. Meditation is a way to quiet your mind and reflect without distraction.

    Self-reflection or introspection is looking within yourself for insight into what makes you unique. However, self-reflection is only part of self-discovery and self-awareness. Looking outward is an important part of learning about yourself. You should ask your trusted social circle to provide feedback or insight into your strengths, weaknesses, and tendencies. Their viewpoint is critical for neutralizing any inherent bias in your self-evaluation. Insight from others can also confirm your self-assessment. I need to emphasize the word "trusted." You need to be careful of who you solicit feedback from. These individuals need to know you well but can give constructive unbiased information. You should include someone from every area of your life to give you a well-rounded view. I know it may be weird to ask people, "what do you think about me," but that's part of the hard work. There's actually a better way to initiate the conversation. You can inform individuals over coffee, email, or text that you are doing some self-improvement work and that you have a few questions you'd like to ask them. Besides, "what are my strong qualities", or "what are the areas where I can improve," you can include questions like, "what do you see as my biggest accomplishment" or "if you were to recommend me for a job, what would you say?." In addition to directly asking others, you gain clues from your interactions like when your friends introduce you, what your professors include in letters of recommendation, or what your supervisor writes in your employee evaluation. Also available are reputable psychological instruments that you can take that provide you with great insight into your preferences, tendencies, and facets of your personality.

Once you have completed your introspection and external evaluation, you'll have a lot of information to process. Look for similarities and differences between your internal reflections and the feedback from your social circle. Decide which qualities may impede your ability to live your life to the fullest which includes personal success and building meaningful connections with others. Decide which of your personal characteristics you would like to keep and strengthen and those characteristics that you need to adapt or minimize.

Your personality traits can be described as a spectrum or a range. I'm carefully using my words, as I do not want to play into the notion that any part of you is bad. The primary goal is to become adaptable in life's situations. Meaning, you can analyze a situation, determine which part of your personality needs to lead and which part needs to take a back seat. For example, if you are outspoken, you may be considered rude because you may not listen well to others. Or you can be seen as an advocate for transparency or justice. If you are trying to negotiate and build rapport with others, you may want to work on active listening. However, you may be the perfect person to be on the front lines of a social justice movement. For me, I have learned that I am extremely compassionate and believe in development and second chances. This comes in handy when I am coaching students and cultivating their potential. I had to pull back on this trait when I became a Higher Education Administrator who supervised more than 20 people and had to make tough management decisions. The budget could not afford my compassion at 100%. I had to let some people go. My middle ground was to give them one chance to improve and provide support for change. If those conditions were not met, I made the ultimate decision. Learning to adapt my personality to situations but hold on to my values was and continues to be challenging at times. Yet, it is a part of adulting.

Our personalities are our default setting, but that does not mean it is our only setting. It is up to you to add and adjust other settings as needed. Being able to evaluate yourself and become self-aware is such a strong skill that employers place it in their top 10 essential workplace skills. When you become more sensitive to your own thoughts and behaviors, you can become more accountable. Taking personal accountability is the foundation for strong relationships between family, friends, and colleagues.

And, strong relationships are critical to success in every area of your life.

Run Diagnostic, Reboot and Update: Processing Emotions and Past Experiences

We are who we are because of our past experiences. Our personality, values, attitude, and beliefs are based in the narrow reality of our childhood and teenage years. Our world was crafted by our teachers, our parents, our family, our friends, the television and the internet. We did not have much control over what influenced us. Whatever we heard or saw--regardless if it was just an instance or if it was constantly--shapes our thoughts and perceptions. All our behavior, actions, and reactions are grounded in our early years. Whatever we were taught became the measuring stick for truth and facts, even if it was inaccurate. Whatever we felt then, positive or negative, stayed with us.

One of the biggest things we were taught is how not to feel. "Oh, don't cry. It's okay." "Don't be sad, it'll get better." When we don't have an opportunity to acknowledge emotions in a safe space, we can't analyze them to find out why we feel that way and what caused us to feel. Even now, a lot of people use the phrase, "I feel some type a way about it." Most times, we can't even identify our emotions. When we don't process emotions, they remain with us, bottled-up and pushed to the corners of our unconscious minds. That means all the times we reacted to situations in our younger years and did not have the chance to figure out our emotions resulted in emotional suppression. Suppressed negative emotions can lead to mental illness like depression, anger, anxiety, but also physical illness. Any unaddressed trauma or pain, no matter how small, plays a huge role in how we see ourselves and relate to others. It is the source of our insecurities and the triggers for our actions and reactions.

To hide our insecurities, we create defensive barriers and survival tactics that prevent others from getting close and seeing us for who we are. These emotional walls inhibit personal connections that lead to any type of relationships (i.e., friendship, family, business, professional). Relationships are the real currency, not money. People who can sustain success over years have mastered the art of building relationships. The first part of mastering relationships is to process your pent-up emotions and heal the hurt. You've probably heard the phrase, "hurt people, hurt people." (I giggle every time I hear it. One of my really interesting friends yelled this out in the middle of an argument with her boyfriend. I'm almost sure it caught him off guard.) Seriously though, this phrase is true. Whenever you feel threatened and you begin to feel just a little like you felt when you were initially hurt, you go into defense mode. You do something to make yourself feel better and/or make them feel worse. Inflicting pain on others is the number one way to ruin a relationship. Yes, inflicting pain could be saying or doing something mean, but you can also hurt others by shutting down communications, not showing respect, or making them feel uncomfortable.

This may seem like a bunch of psychological mumbo jumbo, but just look around you. Think about the most unbearable person you know in your family, on your job, or in your classes. They can be rude, obnoxious, egotistical, and confrontational. The person who argues with everyone is probably dealing with hurt from feeling like they've never been protected or heard so they have to make sure they stick up for themselves and make sure everyone knows what's on their mind. The kid who was bullied is now a fully grown adult and the worst manager ever. He is a micromanager who over asserts his power because he's never dealt with being powerless against his antagonizers.

There are so many adults that are living in the prison of their younger self. They have not processed emotions from trauma in their childhoods. They are rationalizing life based on false information they were fed as a teenager. They are still viewing the world from frames of a very limited reality. This is a miserable and unfortunate way to live because as adults we have control over our reality. We have the power to reframe our perspective on life and get a new happier normal. We have access to multiple sources of information so we can make better decisions and not settle for the "truth" coming from one person. We don't have to see life the way we once did as a child.

Carrying around emotional baggage and limiting beliefs gets heavy. Imagine carrying around that weight until you are 60? Unload it now while you are young. Why? Because there's even heavier things you may have to carry and process later in life. You don't want that extra burden. If you let go of these emotional barriers and learn how to process them now, you'll be stronger, mentally and emotionally. And you'll be in a better position to handle whatever life may throw at you. Challenges in life are, sometimes, consequences of our own actions. Sometimes, trouble is a result of the consequences of the actions of others. Other times, no one is at fault, and trials arise from the natural order of life. Point is, though, do not let life rob you of peace, joy, and prosperity.

So, what does healing look like? How does an emotionally healthy person act? To answer these questions, let's look at the concept of emotional intelligence. Yes, there is more than one type of intelligence. Daniel Goleman coined the phrase "emotional intelligence," defining it as "the ability to identify and manage one's own emotions as well as the emotions of others". This concept came about through observing that there are a lot of smart people who can relate to things and processes but not people. In other words, they have a high IQ but low EQ. Individuals that possess optimal EQ levels embrace change, learn to adapt, are self-aware (sound familiar?), understand others' feelings, disregard perfectionism, keep an open mind and practice gratefulness. Many of these characteristics are also on our Grown-Up Glow Up list. Emotional intelligence is super important for personal and professional success. Earmarking these qualities for areas of continual improvement can only result in a brighter grown-up glow up.

So how do you heal the hurt and increase your emotional intelligence? Let's look at the title of this section, "Run Diagnostic, Reboot, and Update." Originally, I named this section "Reframe your Emotions." I realized it takes a little more than that, hence the change. Computers are intelligent enough that if they begin to malfunction, it will run a diagnostic on itself. Then, when a solution is found and applied, your computer then reboots itself for the fix to occur. And, to prevent future damage, it undergoes regular updates to debug, fix potential issues, and improve performance. Just like our technological companion, we too are intelligent enough to run an emotional and mental self-diagnostic. We need to reset in times where we are malfunctioning. Yes, we malfunction. Those times where we overheat, get overloaded with information, and freeze up. We, too, have a stupid blue screen, when we stop communicating, stop functioning, and stop producing.

Unfortunately, there is no simple Alt, Ctrl, Delete buttons we can push to reboot ourselves. It takes time and hard work to separate our original emotional operating system from bad things that have attached that cause the malfunctions to occur. Viruses create security breaches, make a system vulnerable to other malware, and can cause a computer to crash. Likewise, negative past experiences are just like viruses, they secretly invade our thoughts, hijack our actions, and cultivate our insecurities. Until we run a diagnostic, we likely won't even know we've been emotionally hacked. And, although we hate the time that it takes to update our operating systems, it is a necessity to patch emotional security breaches and update programming to ensure that we are running smoothly and that our internal processes are running at optimal rates.

So, how does this work with real people? First, you must uncover what hurts you, no matter how big or small. Also, identify the source of your thoughts and behaviors. This should be a priority in your self-reflection practices. If you had a traumatic childhood or if you had just one traumatic event that rocked your whole world, you should definitely include that on your list. Be sure to think about any generational habits, thinking, or actions that have been a consistent presence for your family. What has been normalized (good or bad)? Have you been questioning anything from your past? Even if you feel that you've been blessed with a relatively good and normal life, what values do you want to keep or what patterns of thinking do you want to change? Are there any strained relationships you need to resolve? When I say resolve, I don't mean solely reconnect with that person. I mean figure out what it is that caused the strain and decide if that relationship brings enough value to your life that you need to continue it. It is definitely okay to bring resolution by deeming that relationship as toxic and walking away with nothing but well wishes for that person. You must be honest with yourself and double check to make sure you are not the toxic person. These are only a few examples of emotional places to explore. Always continue to question yourself on the reasons you feel, think and act certain ways.

After you identify your hurt, pain, or internal conflict, you must then treat the wounds, resolve the conflict, and gain new perspectives. No matter the size of trauma or the depth of hurt, the service of a mental health professional is always the best option. You're blessed to grow up in an age where therapy is becoming the norm. Take advantage of it. Don't let the stigma of therapy keep you from being emotionally healthy. Our perspective of therapy is the perfect example of things that our past has shaped and things that require reconsideration in light of new information. A trained specialist can help you process your emotions and provide the right support you need while you are at your most vulnerable point. Try pairing therapy with mindfulness practices.

Meditation, self-reflection, journaling, yoga, deep breathing are examples of ways you can relax and focus internally on what you are thinking and feeling. Repeating daily affirmations help you replace old negative thoughts with new ones. Monitoring and improving the way you talk to yourself can assist you in controlling your actions and reactions to situations that trigger negative emotions. Be sure to make forgiveness a primary priority on your journey to healing and emotional wellness. This means forgiving yourself for mistakes and not treating yourself fairly. To forgive those who have wronged you. Unforgiveness is the heaviest bag you can carry with you in life. Lastly, expand your view of the world by reading more and taking time to learn the stories of others. You'd be amazed at how many people have experienced the same tragedies, struggles, and pain as you have. This helps you to not feel alone as well as to help gain a sense of how others have overcome their situation. Understanding the life of others will also help you become more empathetic and grateful for your own struggles and victories.

Mental and emotional wellness is not just a fad. It is imperative that just as you take care of your body, that you take care of the most important part of you, your mind and your soul. Once you are at peace with yourself and have healed your old emotional wounds, you can build genuine relationships with others. Genuine relationships happen when both people are secure in who they are, are not immediately defensive, are not afraid to show their flaws and appreciate the strengths of one another. Authentic relationships are the key to a prosperous life. A great leader leads through relationship building and great leadership is essential to career success. Great marriages are sustained when two emotionally healthy individuals can neutralize the hurt from past relationships, identify and control emotions, and communicate effectively. Once you can resolve childhood conflicts involving your parents, you can raise your children in a healthy environment without the weight of emotional baggage. You don't want to become that old mean, bitter, resentful professor, boss, uncle, or aunt you've encountered. Use your young adult years to intentionally do the internal work to become emotionally whole and mentally well for a prosperous, impactful life.

Living on Purpose: Finding Your Ikigai

Once you have cleared up all the emotional clutter, you've examined your fears, identified your insecurities, and reframed your thinking, you now have more energy and clarity to think bigger and broader than what's in front of you. That bigger broader thing is purpose. You've been searching for it for a long time. You've been trying to figure out your place in life. You thought it was tied tightly to your career and your major, but you still feel a sense of emptiness even after you graduated with your degree. I felt this way for a long time. I had so many things that I wanted to do. I had so many talents I wanted to develop and so many ideas to explore. I was so confused and paralyzed at the thought of trying to reconcile them all. I was an introverted, Christian, STEM major, sorority girl, who loved to tutor, wanted to be a professor and own a business. My disenchantment with my outlook on my life worsened when the original career path of becoming a tenured professor slowly slipped out of range. I felt like I was just working to pay bills. I didn't have enough time or energy at the end of the day to do exactly what I wanted to do to make me happy. What's even crazier is that I had no clue what really made me happy. I was a mess. I was really just existing during the years after graduate school even though I seemed like I had it all. I had three degrees, a job with benefits at a big-name university, a brand-spanking new house, and a car. What else was missing? Me. I was missing. I did everything I was supposed to do. I chased my educational dreams to the very end of the road. I didn't know who I was outside of that. I had yet to truly define my purpose.

I think our culture has taught us that our purpose is connected to our vocation, studies, career, and family. And when there is a snag in one of those things, we lose our sense of self. I encountered a simple concept, *Ikigai*, that forever changed the way I looked at purpose. I have no idea when or how I stumbled upon this philosophy. *Ikigai* is an old Japanese concept. In its simplest form it can best be described in one question, "what's your reason for waking up?" In a more complex view, *Ikigai* is where various aspects of life align. Think about a Venn diagram with multiple overlapping circles, the single convergence of those layers of loops is your *Ikigai*. What makes up your *Ikigai*? There's four major parts to this concept of purpose: 1) What you love 2) What the world needs 3) What you can be paid for 4) What you are good at. Now you see why this concept was life changing for me (hopefully it'll be for you too). The confusion and cognitive dissonance dissipated once I began to understand the layers of ourselves. Now I had a template of sorting out my talents, my education and my passions. Let's take a deeper look into each major component.

The two things that make up what you love are your passion and your mission. Passion is an intense desire or enthusiasm for something. Your personal mission is an important goal or purpose that is accompanied by strong conviction. You can like a lot of things, but you need to look at the trends and patterns of the things you love. Think about the experiences you've had where you are so engrossed that time flies by. You don't even have to go all deep and philosophical with it.

The Concept of Ickigai. Created by Dennis Bodor and Emmy van Deurzen, Wikimedia.

Dr. Erin Wheeler

What TV shows are you drawn to? What news stories catch your eye? What are the causes that you rally behind? What gets on your nerves that no one else can understand? What are things you are willing to do without expectation of compensation?

Here's my take. I am passionate about learning, growing, and evolving. My personal mission is to empower others to overcome any obstacle so that they live the life God intended for them to live. How did I arrive at this (current) conclusion? I am a nerd. I love learning anything and everything. I am a sponge for random facts. I love finding out how things get done. I love processes, especially processes that involve starting from scratch. I love history, especially archaeology. I love movies, but I'm a sucker for behind the scenes and extras. I'm intrigued by stories of trials and triumph. I'm obsessed about beating the odds by superhuman attention to detail and work ethic. I love HGTV, the Food Network, and the History Channel. I like seeing how dilapidated houses become mini mansions with the work of a team. I love seeing cooks take interesting ingredients and build a culinary masterpiece that I'll never be able to taste. I'm a Marvel fan not just because of their amazing special effects and great writing, but also their extraordinary 10-year strategic vision with nearly perfect weaving of details across 20 films and dozens of TV shows. As I'm writing this, Beyonce's *Homecoming* Netflix Special plays in the background. Queen B's work ethic and transparency inspires me, especially her personal story of sacrifices and time invested to make her way back to what she loves. Likewise, I love the Breakfast Club because of their insightful interviews that help the culture to focus on the person behind the music or camera.

Juxtapose all of this to my professional and entrepreneurial endeavors: I am an educator, a success coach, and a tutor. I enjoy seeing first-year college students evolve over the course four years into a college graduate, just like houses evolve on *Flip or Flop*. I love to help someone who feels like building a business, finding a job, or writing a book is impossible through the process of getting what they want. I love breaking down a challenging concept and engaging students in learning so that they can feel more confident in their ability as a scholar. I enjoy sharing information that I feel can improve the quality of life and encouraging others to embrace lifelong learning. It makes me happy when people win and succeed. I can transfer this love of empowerment and education to any context and still enjoy it.

The clues for what you love are all around you. You must pause, observe, and analyze the things that you do every day. Take the time to form your own personal mission statement. It is one of the activities that I do with freshman seminar classes and productivity retreats for professionals. It helps to put things into perspective and helps you to stay focused in times of challenge. Your personal mission statement will evolve as your life experiences change. Creating one now, however, will help you get to your next phase in life.

In continuing our exploration of *Ikigai*, let's break down the concept of what the world needs. A ton of problems exist in the world around you. It is impossible to expect any single person to fix it all. Yet, each person can contribute a piece of the solution. Combining your mission with your vocation helps you to address a piece of what the world needs. We've talked about mission. Let's dive into vocation. Your vocation is an inclination for a certain type of work. It's your calling. I'd like to think of this as something that comes naturally to you. Something that you don't need much training for or something you can pick up quickly. This intersection of mission and vocation provides an excitement and fulfilment that comes from positively impacting the world. The world doesn't have to include all the continents. Your world could be scaled down to your community, your neighborhood, or your family. What is something that you think the world needs? Is there a particular group of people that you have empathy for that you wish you could help? What is your solution to the problem?

Let's move from what the world needs and bring this back to you. What about what you need? Helping your world improve may bring excitement. But can it help you pay the bills? Moving a little further into the concept of *Ikigai*, you find that the combination between profession and vocation provides some insight into this question. You may be asking, how's vocation different than profession? So, I do have to admit that when I first started researching this topic, I was confused between the terms "vocation" and "profession." Above, we discussed your vocation as a tendency to be drawn to a certain type of work. Your profession is work that requires specialized training and is defined by a series of jobs over time. My interpretation (there's many on this subject) is that the difference in vocation and profession is training and the consistency over time. Combining the aspects of profession and vocation creates something that you can get paid for. However, just working without any aspect of passion or mission leaves you feeling empty.

Passion and profession mesh to give us what we are good at. When these two areas line up, you may feel a sense of fulfillment, but this fulfillment may be superficial. You may question your results and success in your profession. Am I really making a difference? Is my work really helping people and solving real problems?

As you can see, focusing on a single element of *Ikigai* almost certainly leads to lacking something: money, legacy, impact, fulfillment, satisfaction, stability. The reason that this concept brought so much value to me, was that it helped me put life into perspective. It helped me to see that pretty much everyone is looking for that sweet spot in life where you are spending everyday doing what you love while making an impact that brings meaning to your life and not having to sacrifice the quality of life to do it. It helped me to adjust my expectations that my 9-5 job wasn't meant to provide me with 100% everything that I needed, but it had a significant purpose in my life. Therefore, I acknowledge what it was and was grateful that my job provided me with a salary, experience and network. All the other things that I found lacking, I no longer complained about or got depressed over. I took the time to reflect on what I wanted and what I needed to be happy. I wanted to be heard. I wanted to see my effort directly tied to results, albeit good or bad. I wanted to be creative and innovative without the bureaucracy of Higher Education. I wanted to directly impact my community and address the problems of college success at the root. I began to seek other outlets to fill the gap that my job couldn't. That's when I leaned into my hustle and my own ideas. I began the leg work to create my own non-profit. These combination of owning my own education-based business and a non-profit helped to lead me closer to my *Ikigai*. It aligned with my passion, vocation, mission, and financial goals. Adding in and prioritizing my involvement with my church and sorority, definitely gave me a fuller picture of my purpose and the things that made me happy. Your path to *Ikigai* will be different from mine. You may find that your combination may be a 9-5 as financial investor and a hobby as a singer. Even as you mature and evolve, your center of fulfillment will evolve as well. As you accomplish and experience things in life, you will have to re-ignite your passion, refine your mission, re-evaluate your profession and find new vocations. Not to mention that the world changes so fast that new needs are created every day.

One last thing. Don't confuse contentment with an easy life. Even when you find your *Ikigai*, life will still bring about challenges to get you out of alignment and cause you to question your path and your purpose. You have to find a way to be content and confident in your purpose in the face of trials. Yes, being an entrepreneur is hard. Yes, your 9-5 will work all your nerves. Yes, there will never be enough resources to achieve your dreams. However, the assuredness in your purpose will help you fight through when you're tired and defeated. You may even quit a few times. But, you know that it's your true purpose and part of your *Ikigai*, when you are drawn back to it like a magnet. Yes, I have walked away from my non-profit and my business, and my profession many times. Even as I type, the coronavirus crisis has totally put a damper on the summer camp I am fighting to consistently host each year in the wake of my new job and slew of life changes. I've vacillated a hundred times to cancel it, all the while still putting together an action plan to make it work. Finding your purpose may be easier than staying true to it. I truly believe that knowing what you should be doing and not doing it will lead to the most miserable and uncomfortable existence ever. So, find your *Ikigai*, get comfortable in that sweet spot, and don't succumb to the pressures of life and deviate from your path.

Don't just take my word for it. I can share with you inspiring stories from two of my closest friends, Domonique and Phaon. Domonique and I met in undergrad. We both bonded over our church girl ways and desire to experience college in its fullest without compromising ourselves. *Pats self on the back* I can say we did. After college, we moved into an apartment in her hometown of Baton Rouge where she worked for an afterschool program, and I began my graduate program at Southern University. Now working for an after-school program was not in her top job choices, but it tapped into her natural talents for working with kids. She is a kid magnet, and she was a natural teacher. She became the official youth pastor of the church founded by her parents a few years after she graduated college. Not only is she great with kids and teens, but she is also super creative. She can dance, write and recite poetry, paint, draw, and pretty much anything creative. While a case could be made that growing up in church and her communications degree helped her to be a great speaker, I would argue that motivating others through words is a God-given ability. Most majors dream to be on TV or Radio or a chance to be the next Olivia Pope. However, Domonique's ultimate goal was to work full-time in ministry. Like most of our post-college dreams, this goal was not realized. She did what she had to until she was able to support herself full-time in ministry. Her program manager job provided just enough money and fulfillment for her for a few years after college.

Like many college graduates in 2007, we were subject to jobs disappearing right from under us.

Domonique's non-profit program was cut because of funding. This was a rough period for her, she was definitely trying to find herself and her purpose in the absence of opportunity to do what she truly wanted to do. However, opportunity came knocking in a form of a teaching position in a local Christian school. I can remember when she called and told me the news, I think I was more excited for her than she was. I thought it was so perfect for her. I took her back to her original, slightly altered, goal of working full-time in ministry. In this position, she could combine all the gifts she had inside, and she didn't have to hide her light or be broke. This was the moment I saw the glow from her Grown-Up Glow-Up translated into *Ikigai* speak, her passion aligned with her mission, her profession, and her vocation. Guess what? She's still at the same school with a cooler position, Campus Pastor. Not only is able to teach the Word of God, but she also still gets to impact kids. I was super excited for her when she told me about the promotion. The enjoyment and fulfillment she experienced opened her mind to other possibilities. After her promotion, she called me and said she realized that there are so many other interesting positions that she can consider in her career like being the chaplain of major league sports teams or campus pastors at universities. Domonique is the perfect example of keeping the faith in finding a way to make a living while living out your purpose.

So, it wasn't a great stretch of imagination to see a communications major use her degree to support her in teaching, preaching, and speaking. However, in Phaon's case, it is hard to imagine a biology major ultimately leading up his own creative agency. I also met Phaon during undergrad. He was also my boyfriend. I was an introverted social butterfly, but he was definitely more outgoing that I was. Like many African American males, he was focused on getting to the money. He had his hopes set on becoming a pharmacist with his biology degree

Alas, Phaon found his passion in party promotion. He and his friends through really great parties. At the time, I just thought it was just a college hobby. I was antsy about him risking money on upfront costs and all, but it always seems to pan out. He even was part of bringing notable guest to campus and surrounding cities like Fonzworth Bentley (I know that name may not strike any excitement with you, but he was really popular because of his work with P. Diddy, Diddy, Puff Daddy or however you identify the person known as Sean "Puffy" Combs.) I think he even organized events featuring Rick Ross and Drake right before they blew up the charts in 2006 and 2007. I was uninterested in either of those parties, 'cause who wanted to hear the guy from Degrassi rap? Okay, looking back, I feel stupid. But, Phaon always had a pulse on what's hot and trendy culture before everyone else knew. As his success with event planning and promotion grew, his interest in his pharmacy waned. He tried to hold fast to it for a while, he even began his pre-requisites at Texas Southern University. He ultimately lost all passion for Pharmacy and moved back to Louisiana to finish his biology degree because he was too deep in to change majors. After college, he moved to New York to find himself. He dabbled in acting for a while. He eventually found himself working for a non-profit that actually was an initiative of President Obama's My Brother's Keeper Program. There he used what he knew: event planning, and promotion. He was able to connect the African American male community to important resources to help them become better fathers and men. His ability to make anything seem hot and trendy helped the program meet its goals. His eye for fashion and aesthetics contributed to making sure the website and other marketing tools stayed up to date. And his ability to learn difficult material (aka biology) helped him to become a savvy, self-made marketing expert. He eventually took his talents to the multi-cultural marketing division in a major fortune 500 company. For me, this is when he began his Glow Up. He then leveraged his knack for throwing parties into becoming an experiential marketer who creates amazing events to promote products and services. After his time ended with the company, he decided to open his own creative agency which he officially launched just days prior to me penning this chapter. Both Phaon and Domonique are inspirations to me in how they were bold enough to cast away conventional thinking, follow their hearts with clear logic and go for what makes them fulfilled. I don't know how I am surrounded by super creative people, but he was also creative like Domonique. Come to think of it, they grew down the street from each other. (This is totally a coincidence that I chose these to friends to discuss.)

To obtain your Grown-Up, Glo-Up, you must be intentional. It is so easy to say you are finding yourself, only to find yourself on the couch binging Netflix. Personal development requires strategic effort. You must be intrinsically motivated to do the work. What does this look like? Now, you don't have to post on social media that you are "working on yourself." You do, however, want to set aside a period of time where you are doubling down, focusing, and actually doing the work. While self-discovery and growing is a continuum, you need to take significant strides early on to get to a place of balance, peace and enlightenment. During your time of personal discovery and growth, you should be setting personal goals and linking them to specific actions and outcomes. Here are some things that count as being intentional about your personal development and glowing up:

- Practicing meditation.
- Buying a journal and scheduling time to write.
- Finding a therapist or counselor, scheduling and attending a series of sessions.
- Volunteering in places where you think your passions may lie.

- Reading books, completing courses, and listening to podcasts on topics related to your strengths, weaknesses, and interests.
- Completing informational interviews with people who are doing things that interest you.
- Working with a success and or a career coach.
- Attending church regularly.
- Creating your mission statement.
- Holding conversations with your trusted circle about your strengths and weaknesses.
- Completing personality and strengths-based surveys and self-assessments.
- Keeping a list of habits you want to change and intentionally doing the work to change them.
- Having conversations with people who have hurt you and with people you've hurt to apologize, forgive, move on or move ahead.
- Cultivating and rebuilding relationships with others who you have deemed worthy.
- Trying new things that get you out of your comfort zone.
- Testing out things that make you happy.
- Reflecting, exploring, and journaling through the elements of *Ikigai*.

Being a Glowed-Up Grown-Up, is all about finding your *Ikigai* and gaining control over every area of life. Understanding yourself helps you to live authentically. Improving your mental and emotional health helps you to be a better employee, co-worker, sibling, child, spouse, friend, and parent. Once you find your *Ikigai* you are able to make better decisions regarding your time and focus. Getting rid of emotional weight, falling in love with yourself, and living out your purpose leads to unconditional happiness. You'll have a solid mental and emotional core that will have you glowing and growing in the right direction no matter what adulting may throw at you.

FLOW AND GO

Live Wiser

FLOW AND GO

Adulting is hard.

I think I've said that before. But, it's worth repeating again.

Adulting is hard!

*

Through my careful observations, for the last 15-20 years ('Ish didn't get real until I was 24), I've identified the top four reasons adulting sucks.

Reason #1: Freedom is a double-edged sword. When we were young, all we wanted was to be grown. Why? Because we were under the impression that we could do anything we wanted to and that we wouldn't have to listen to anyone. We thought being an adult was so sexy. We could eat what we wanted, go where we wanted, hang out with who we wanted, and wear what we wanted. We all heard "don't grow up too fast" or "You have your whole life to be an adult." We didn't understand why adults said this until we were knee-deep into adulthood. They were warning us against the other side of the sword, perhaps the sharpest side: being accountable for the outcomes of our actions. The beauty of adulthood is that you absolutely have free reign over your life. You can do whatever you like. You can take all the credit for when things go right, but you have no one else to blame when things go wrong.

It's all on you.

Reason #2: Decisions, decisions, decisions.
As kids, we would get so frustrated that much of life was already decided: bedtime, meals, clothes, schedules. So much so that I would be excited when my parents would ask what flavored Kool-Aid I wanted to drink. We were so focused on the disregard for our preferences and choices that we became obsessed about the day we could make our own choices. But the choices we were so focused on making on our own were so simple. We all couldn't wait to watch rated-R movies, eat in our rooms, eat the cake before dinner, not eat vegetables, and to eat McDonald's every day.

Dr. Erin Wheeler

I don't know about you, but I felt like my parents were the strictest ever. I really didn't have many choices. Even when they put it in the form of a question, I knew they were really just trying to be nice. It was really petty of them, because my answer really didn't matter. "You like this shirt?" "Not really." "You need some more church shirts and it's on sale." "Okay." Shirt purchased. Even with the decisions I could make, like being a good student or picking my friends, I didn't really make them on my own. My parents were always in my head. Since they put the fear of God in me, I was really afraid to make any risky decisions.

My dad, my grandfather, and my uncle were all bus drivers, so they knew everyone. And everybody knew them. Added to the equation was Mr. Ervin, a deacon at my church who was also the head of facilities at my elementary, middle, and high schools. He kept me and all my other church friends in check, because he, too, knew everything and everybody and everybody knew him. My parents always had eyes and ears on me at all times throughout K-12. If I breathed wrong, they found out. If I snuck and had a few "Lil friends" (friend-boys never boyfriends), they found out. If I spent too much time with the fast or rowdy girls, they found out. I surrendered in middle school when I realized that I couldn't get away with anything and simply defaulted to doing what I was told to do. To me, that wasn't a choice. It was forced compliance. Since someone else made my choices for me, I was bursting at the seams to graduate, go to college, and get out of the house to do my own thing and make my own choices.

I really thought my parents were still going to be strict and over-bearing even when I got to college. I was braced for it. I'm still bracing for it. On my freshman move-in day, they set up my dorm room, kissed me goodbye, and told me to ring the doorbell before using my key when I came to home to visit (they swear they never said that). They never came back to visit me on campus. That day marked the first day I truly felt like an adult. It was so scary. My very protective, very strict parents had released me to do my own thing and make my own choices. I feel like that was the last time they decided anything for me. If they gave me space and freedom right after high-school graduation, they certainly gave me a whole lot of space and opportunity after college graduation.

This is when I certainly felt the pressure to make tough calls for myself. Now, I was facing real adult decisions.

Looking back, all the choices and tough decisions I had to make in college paled in comparison. The magnitude and the number of tough decisions exponentially increased post-grad. Now there were choices between PPO's and HMO's; whole life and term life; high premiums and low deductibles; IRAs versus 401ks. Don't even mention the decisions you have to make when your paycheck doesn't match your lifestyle. While I did have the luxury of asking my parents their advice, I had to make the final decision. I thought for sure they would have a definitive "yes" or "no" when I wanted to buy a house. They didn't. They gave the "just pray on it" speech. Now what they did absolutely say "no" to was me coming back home for six months to save money for a down payment. That was "a no and God will work it out."

I did decide to buy a house. I was very much on my own with the process, because my parents were really blessed to own a home that they didn't have to search for. Our cousin built a brand-new house next door to my grandparents when she suddenly had to move. My grandfather convinced my incredibly young parents to buy it. Because of this, my parents couldn't provide advice for the house hunting process based on experience. I was blessed in my own way to have my best friend's mom, a realtor, guide me through the process. Buying a house ended up being way easier than I thought. I don't even remember looking at many houses before I settled on the one I purchased. However, my toughest call was related to buying a home, but not in the way you think.

I started the process of buying my home in June 2011. My grandmother suddenly passed the day I was supposed to close the purchase (the closing was rescheduled). A few days later, my dad told me that she had left me her house and asked if I wanted to go through with purchasing my own home. That was the biggest choice. He didn't pressure me. It was a two-minute conversation, but the weight of that decision still lingers with me. It was my decision alone to make. No one really could even provide any advice to me. My grandmother had visited the home when I was in the buying process. She was so proud of me. I didn't know that was one of the last few moments I would spend with her. However, I knew she always reminded me that I had a home, her home. I ultimately decided it was too soon to move in her house. Emotionally, I couldn't take it. Although it would have been really great financially to have a house without a mortgage, I just couldn't do it. If I wasn't so close to closing and I had taken a moment to process it more, I may have chosen differently. Alas, there was no time.

The next day after I talked to my dad, I closed on my house. I was only 26. I'm now 35. Making hard decisions that majorly impact your life is commonplace and still hard as hell. The decision to pass up a virtually free house ranks in the top ten of WTF IS LIFE moments. What else is in my top ten tough calls? Hmmm? Let's see. How about moving to Kentucky for a job on some YOLO type life. Then, deciding to be okay with the possibility of getting let go from said job (more about that in the career chapter). There's the choice of not accepting job offers when I haven't worked in a year or two. I think the choice that takes the top spot is choosing whether or not to let my home go into foreclosure and/or file for bankruptcy after my home was flooded and I lost my job. Hard decisions like these are the hallmark of adulting and will always have you saying, "this ish is for the birds." (Email me when you find yourself saying it.) Adulting type decisions make you wish you could go back to a naive childhood. These days, I wish someone would order me to take a nap at 11:00 in the morning and force me to bed at 8:00 PM after someone else cooked dinner and made me eat my vegetables.

Reason #3: Decisions alone aren't what make adulting challenging.

The hardest part comes after the decisions have been made. Being an adult and standing on your own means you can make any choice you want, but you have to be responsible for the outcome. It's easy to deal with good outcomes. It's the consequences that are the hardest to handle. You have to make decisions about everything as an adult, and there's a constant reverberation of repercussions of all sizes. There are little consequences that happen when you choose to eat ice cream (Oreo and Reese's Blast from Sonic is my favorite) and you know you are lactose intolerant. Side effects of that choice are usually temporary and minimal. Then, there are those really big "I f&%ked up moments." These are the times where the effects of your decisions are long-term and impact is wide-spread. No matter the magnitude of the outcome you have to hold yourself accountable.

Holding yourself accountable means holding up the mirror and admitting you made a mistake. Admitting you made a wrong decision sounds easy, but it is the hardest thing in the world. For one, who wants to be honest enough to say they are less than perfect? We've been conditioned to think that adults make all the right decisions. So, when you make an unwise choice which leads to less than positive outcomes, you feel horrible. Complicating things is the embarrassment you feel when your choices begin to affect your public image, and everyone sees the embodiment of your choices.

How you handle the consequences of your actions defines your level of maturity. The one thing that I hate is to see a "grown person" mad about a mistake they've made. Blaming everyone except themselves and expecting others to participate in righting the wrong. Reflecting on your missteps, admitting to yourself that you made the wrong choices, and taking action to resolve the fallout is the gold medal of adulting. Humbleness and accountability are two traits that are the hardest to obtain but are the most valuable qualities you can have. Putting aside my pride and admitting when I have messed up has helped me to rise in my career and garner respect as a leader. I have found that potentially hard conversations go better when you 'fess up. It actually stuns people, especially the "haters." I can remember a time where I was rolling out a significant policy change. I had the support of all the senior leadership including department chairs. I didn't speak directly with faculty because I assumed that their respective department chairs would discuss it with them. When the official memo was released, I could feel the heat emitting from my inbox. It was filled with all kinds of negative responses from faculty. LOL. Who was silent? The people who I thought supported the change in the first place. While I could blame them, I did some self-reflection and realized that I skipped the step of directly speaking with faculty, because, deep down, I really didn't want the battle.

But, I got it anyway.

In the end, I ultimately admitted my mistake and asked for their collegial forgiveness. It was hard conceding, but I had to do what I had to do. When I did admit my mistake, they couldn't say anything. They had their arguments ready and didn't have to use them. They were really shocked that I did that, but act of admitting fault garnered their respect.

Admitting my faults readily wasn't always easy for me. I was always the "smartest in the room." The person who thought a "B" would ruin her life and the girl who fought for a perfect GPA in high school. Me? Admit I was wrong? Chile, please! I would follow you into a lion's mouth to prove I was right. After all, I was the good girl. I didn't make mistakes. I honestly can't pinpoint a significant experience that propelled my growth in this area. I think between my scientific training and my study of entrepreneurship, I was always exposing myself to lessons in failure. Science taught me to always identify where the experiment went wrong and propose fixes for the next experiment. Lessons in start-ups taught me that all businesses fail at least once. And, that all businesses who turn it around have CEOs who are transparent in showing their faults as a leader and propose actions to rectify. Being accountable for your actions is tough. The fear of embarrassment and the pain of learning you're less than perfect makes this challenging.

Reason #4: It's lonely.

The perk of finding your purpose and passion is that you can be happy and satisfied. However, staying true to yourself and your purpose is a table for one. No one can live your life except you. You are the only person who knows what's best for you. If you think your parents can be counted as knowing what's best, see Reason #3. They can tell you what to do, but they can't be held accountable. You are solely responsible for your life. Your friends may be in lanes in your journey of life, but you, my friend, stand in your own lane. This makes adulting tough. All the weight of making decisions and the burden of dealing with consequences rest squarely on your back. It's heavy. But, that is the cost of freedom. You will literally go insane trying to normalize yourself or do whatever everyone wants you to do. This is easier said than done as society, family, and friends are constantly feeding us ideas of what we should be and do. Peer pressure and wanting to fit in doesn't go away once you reach the age of 21. Adulting requires the courage to stand in your own individuality and live a life that is right for you. In the end, it's just you who is bearing the weight of your choices. Everyone will have opinions about your life, but no one will actually bear the burdens for you.

Overcoming loneliness took me a long time to do. But, in order to stand out and achieve what you want, you have to do it alone. Grad school and entrepreneurship has really helped me to get used to standing in my own light. Both of these endeavors required extreme sacrifices. Because writing my dissertation needed my undivided attention, I couldn't go out for 2 for 1 Tuesdays, Happy Hour on Fridays, the hole in the wall on Saturday, and church on Sunday. I could not make every birthday party and all the random shenanigans my friends were doing. I couldn't even enjoy holidays with my family 100% because I used every minute to write. But, I ultimately finished two advanced degrees in four years. And, I didn't miss out on anything.

Likewise, owning and boot-strapping my own business prevented me from buying like everyone else. I had to decide that I was going to pay off my car and drive it as long as I could, while my crew was getting new cars all the time. I couldn't go out to eat every week. I picked my outings accordingly and budgeted my entertainment dollars wisely. Even after I finished my PhD, I still couldn't spend copious amounts of my free time hanging out. I used the evenings and weekends to build my website on my own or teach ACT Prep workshops. Again, I found myself by myself most of the time. It did feel lonely a lot. But, I got through it by continually focusing on my goals and purpose.

    Honestly, I don't think you'll ever fully get over the loneliness of adulting. I still get the feeling when I have to make hard decisions on my own. You may have found yourself laughing at your parents when they talked out loud to themselves. I now know why they did it. Adulting makes you do that. In order to adapt to being alone, you become the second person in your life. You become your own companion even when you are married. You talk to yourself because possibly you are the only one that will listen to and talk back. I do this. It is now a regular practice. (When you find yourself doing this tag me on IG. You've officially entered adulthood).

I'll say this for the third time, adulting is hard. There's not much you can do about life's challenges. Everyone that's breathing experiences trials. You can't change this fact. However, in order to survive the hood called adulting, you have to gain the right perspective. Your mindset is the only thing is you can control. Having the right mindset about life can not only help you survive but also thrive on purpose. I'm not saying this is the only way to view adulting, but here's my take.

The River Mentality

> Don't go chasing waterfalls
> Please stick to the rivers and the lakes that you're used to
> I know that you're gonna have it your way or nothing at all
> But I think you're moving too fast
> -Waterfalls by TLC-

Good songs usually have a water metaphor about life. TLC taught us that waterfalls were analogous to the fast and risky life and that we should stick to the straight and narrow, which were the lakes and rivers.

The fabulous Tina Turner told us to not let the challenges of life get us down and that we should keep rolling like the steamboats on the Mississippi. THE Miss Toni Braxton encouraged us to get it together, let the pain and heartbreak go, and just let it flow. She promised that everything will work out fine. These songs are the soundtrack of my life. Together, they describe my adulting outlook to which I subscribe. I view life like a river on which I keep rolling and drift with the flow. While TLC does recommend sticking to both lakes and rivers, I suggest that in the world of adulting, rivers are superior to lakes in that a lake mentality has its limits. I'll explain.

A lake is an area filled with still water and surrounded by land. Lakes can be man-made or natural. In contrast, a river is a body of freshwater that is not enclosed by land. While a lake's water remains stagnant, a river moves, dynamically, in one direction. If you treat life like a lake, you'll always place boundaries and limitations on yourself. You'll also find yourself going in circles and remaining in the same place no matter what you do because lakes are stagnant and have no movement in any direction.

Because lakes can be made by man, you'll constantly measure your life by standards set by someone else. If you are a river person like me, you see life as one long journey that is unique. You appreciate and expect the twists and turns in life, just like riverboat pilots chart the twists and bends of a river. No one can control life, and no one can (safely) control rivers. You just have to enjoy the ride life takes you on and take advantage of where the waters take you. Like life itself, rivers hold a great deal of potential energy that can be harnessed for good. You can either be a motionless lake, and let adulting paralyze you. Or, you can be a roaring river, giving life to everything in your path.

I didn't formalize this mindset until someone asked me a question that stopped me in my tracks: "Dr. Wheeler, can you give me career advice?" *Blank stare* "I-I-I have nothing to give you," I stuttered. They were just as stunned as I was. Here I was the Assistant Provost of a university at 30 and I had not one piece of advice to give. I never planned anything I accomplished. I just mastered every opportunity I was given and waited until the next one appeared. At that moment, I realized that I literally just drifted from one opportunity to another. I said "yes" to one thing. Made the best of that situation. Then I said, "yes" to something else. My "yes" was my raft, and I just floated from one thing to the other. I honestly couldn't have planned it any better. I actually tried. My plan got me nowhere. In the end, I eventually told the person who requested the advice that even though I'm probably not the person to get career advice from, I had learned to be open to opportunities. Pencil in a plan, but always have your eraser ready to make changes. I didn't know then that what I was describing was the river mentality. But since my life became a white-water rafting trip shortly after this question was posed to me, I had the time and opportunity to flesh out the concept. Let's explore this river mentality a little bit more.

Rivers move in a single direction.

Life is a continuum. From the minute we're born, we are headed towards death. These are facts. It's hard to swim upstream or swim back to the start of the river. Fish master swimming upstream because they are naturally programmed for reproductive purposes. Swimming upstream for us is living in the past and floundering in regret. It takes entirely too much energy to fight against the force of the life that opposes you. Life is always trying to move us forward. Whether its white- water rapids or a lazy river, riding the waves saves you energy as all you have to do is hold on and let the waters carry you from one stop to the next. Going with the flow of life can save you lots of time, energy, and regret.

Flow is important.

Life is about ebbs and flows. The same goes for rivers. The flow for rivers has two components. The first is the amount of water in the river. Rivers can flow all year long or they can dry up and stop flowing for months. There will always be times where life is going well and there's a constant flow of health, love, money, and fun. At some point you may feel as if your world stops and there's a lack of growth, support, and confidence. The amount of water in the rivers also depends on its tributaries. A tributary is a river that feeds into another river, rather than ending in a lake, pond, or ocean. You have to be cautious of who's pouring into you or the quality of sources that are feeding the flow of your life. Are you constantly around negative people? Are you relying on lake people, whose water never moves, to contribute to your flow? Are you investing in yourself? What are you listening to? Who's draining your energy? All of the answers to these questions lie within your authority to change. You have to always use your authority and freedom as an adult to control your environment as everything around you can impact the flow of your life.

The second component of flow is the movement of water. Rivers have proven over time to be a force of nature. Rivers are going to exactly do what they want to--flow. For centuries, humans have tried to tame rivers, much to the peril of those who lived on the banks. An active river will always have movement in its waters. This movement can be like wild rapids, or they can be a gentle stream. Just like the river, you have to keep moving. You have to go with the flow. But not just any flow, *your* flow. Each river has its own unique flow. A river may be shallow in one place and deep in another. It may flow faster in one place and slowly creep in another area. This is the pulse of the river, natural ups, and downs, a natural rhythm.

You have to find the natural flow of your life. This is the hardest part. Why? Because society has pretty much standardized the flow of adulthood. How? They have convinced us the gold standard of adulting is to get a "good job" after graduating. You should stay on that "good job" for four years or as long as you can to show some stability. Meanwhile, you should date with the purpose of settling down. Once you find someone, you should date for at least two years, get engaged, and wait a year before getting married. Within 1-2 years, you should start trying to have kids. If you don't, people will start to ask questions because things are not going according to *their* plans. You should have two kids, a girl and a boy, to make things perfect. Stopping at one is a disservice to your child because you are robbing them of a natural life companion. Having more than two kids makes you look irresponsible. By the time the second child arrives you should be closing on your home, because no one can raise a family in an apartment. Now that you have a good job, a spouse, two kids, a house, and a dog, you can receive the gold medal in the adulting Olympics. Congratulations!

CHURCH ANNOUNCEMENT:

Do not subscribe to this craziness! Thank you. And govern yourselves accordingly.

The belief that adulthood has to flow this way leads to post-grad depression. This belief is false and full of misguiding assumptions. Life, like a river, is not a straight line. Riverboat pilots in the 1800s thought so and they crashed horribly. Believing the life-is-straight theory causes us to buckle under pressure when the course is different from the map, instead of preparing to take a different route. The moment things don't align with this preconceived notion of adulthood, you feel like your whole world has shifted, that your river has run completely dry or your boat has crashed into the banks. This is where movement is important. You have to feel your flow and keep going. You have to do what's best for you. Again, the hardest part of adulting is bearing the burden of responsibility for every decision you make. Forcing yourself to make decisions based on everybody's else views is like damming a river--that ish rarely turns out right.

Some of the worst floods in human history have been caused by trying to make a river flow differently from its natural path or diverting water from its sources. Dams were used to benefit everyone else except the river. If humans wanted to live on a riverbank, they would dam it to decrease flow and prevent flooding. If they wanted a source of electricity, they would dam it to collect the potential energy. No matter how strong dams are built, they are no match for nature. Rivers will always exceed their land barriers or their limitations by not only bursting the dams but also creating new courses. Rivers don't care if there's a community of people who have settled on the banks. A river will still flood a thousand acres. A river will flow where, when and how it wants. You can succeed where, when, and how you want, despite the odds and limitations life presents. You have to view life as a dynamic experience. You have to be flexible and live without limitations. You have to find your signature flow and not dam yourself to fit society's norms. Doing this robs you of your potential, steers you away from your purpose, diverts you away from your purpose, flooding those near you with hurt. (Remember: hurt people hurt people.)

What's one way to chart your own path and keep your flow? Timing is everything, but you can't use the world's master clock. There is no universal set time for life. You have to use your own clock. Yes, ladies you may have a biological clock in which governs reproduction. Yes, guys you have an age in which being a bachelor is taboo. But there is a time in which you are ready to take on the responsibility outcomes of the decisions you make. It's never an age, but a state of maturity or readiness that makes the timing right. Many times, we want something, but we aren't really ready to handle it. If you aren't ready (mentally, emotionally, and financially) to handle any commitment and responsibility of major decisions, don't do it.

The second way to keep the flow, is to trust your instinct and follow your intuition. These are the two natural abilities that underscore our purpose. However, fear of being an outlier, an embarrassment, or a failure buries both our instinct and intuition. Deep down, we know the choices we should make in life. Yet, we don't listen to our internal voice and we don't feel the pulse of our life. We choose to dam and oppose our unique flow. I've observed my friends fall into this trap. *Sidenote: I am not saying that I didn't make the same mistakes they did, I had the opportunity to see how their decisions turned out before I had the chance to make similar choices. I excelled in academics, but I was socially delayed. I took my time dating and I didn't rush to have sex. Thus, stalling a lot of the major decisions I had to make about marriage and family.*

Back to the timing trap. I've had some college friends marry their high school sweetheart because they had been together for nearly 10 years and it was the natural step to take because they graduated college. In 99% of the situations, they knew it wouldn't work, but they ignored their instinct and got married anyway only to divorce a year later. I've witnessed others force themselves into relationships because they felt as if they needed to be married with kids at a certain age, so they married the person they were with when they turned 25. They disregarded the signs and dismissed their intuition and proceeded to make a choice based on an arbitrary rule instead of waiting until the right person came along. They may have been financially ready to begin a family, but they were not emotionally ready for a huge commitment.

Outside of marriage and family, I've observed other friends ignore their instinct to follow their true purpose and instead opt for a job that allowed them to paint a superficial picture of success. In all of these scenarios, my friends suffered traumatic consequences. It took them years to work through regret and pain to find themselves again. It takes courage to make a decision for yourself and stand by it. It takes even more to let your life play out in front of others.

I am a major believer that if you follow your instincts, stick to your purpose, and stay open to opportunity, your life will flow into place. I am glad that I am an extraordinarily strong introvert. I observe everything around me. I also don't make hasty decisions. I have to investigate the situation from all angles. So, me seeing my friends' and families' experiences (good and bad) with marriage caused me to pause and really reflect on what I wanted out of life. At first, I subscribed to the notion of the standard life (married by 25, child by 30). Well, it didn't work out.

I really had a vision of my boyfriend proposing to me outside on the yard at SUBR after we both graduated with our PhD's. *I'm laughing so hard typing this.* It was really clear as day. We would have engagement pictures by the entrance and have a chance to be in *Ebony* magazine. We would be the picture of black educated love. NONE OF THIS HAPPENED! Things didn't work out. I had a chance to force an engagement, but I just let the natural course of life take place and my intuition take over. That's when I realized I didn't want that life bad enough. What's so funny to me, looking back, I wasn't ready to be anybody's wife and definitely nobody's mom. Some may call it selfish but it really was the best form of self-care. I was more focused on living the life of CEO of my own company and building a career in education to complement. I wanted the freedom to travel, to buy fly stuff, to have my own home, and to do what I wanted to do. I followed my gut to follow the trail of opportunities that presented itself to me.

I think in an alternate dimension, the married me would have been stuck trying to make my career dreams work at my first job that had a very low ceiling. I would probably have to say no to the job in Kentucky that changed my life. If I would have been able to take the job with a husband and kid in tow, I definitely would have been pressured to stay in a toxic work environment so as to not disrupt the stability of my family. Coming home to an empty house was a luxury to me after a long workday on that job. I don't know if I could handle that position and accomplish as much as I did if I would have had a family. I doubt you would be reading this book. I just think my life would have been totally different had I went against my instinct and forced myself into a life meant for someone else. We can always want something in life, but it doesn't mean that it's something we need. And, it doesn't mean that need has to be met at that moment.

I'm not saying marriage and family are out of the cards for me. I'm only saying that I remain grateful for where I am in life. I am enjoying my journey. I'm not going to let some arbitrary rules of society interrupt my flow. I am not going to make decisions I have to live with because people are asking questions about my lifestyle. When someone special comes along who is worthy of my time and attention, I am going to take it day by day. I am going to follow my instinct. If it leads me down the aisle, I'll be ecstatic. When and if we are ready to have kids, we'll see what my ovaries say, if not, I'll adopt, find a surrogate, or just continue on being a great aunt and godmother. I will just go with the flow. I will give everything 100% so I'll have no regrets. But, if things don't go as "planned," I'll just keep moving forward. It's easier said than done, but my go with the flow attitude has helped me navigate adulthood thus far.

> *The Mississippi River will always have its own way; no engineering skill can persuade it to do otherwise... - Mark Twain.*

Rivers change continuously.

A river may move in a single direction but it's the path to its destination or the river delta changes often. The flow of the river at any point may pick up debris or deposit sediment, widening or narrowing passages along the way. In the 1800s, when the new world was still "discovering the mysteries of the Mississippi River, confident riverboat pilots would often crash their boats. These accidents would happen because pilots assumed the course, they charted would remain the same. After the consistent death of passengers and crews, pilots began to brace for the changes to the river. They adapted to evolving conditions by re-learning the river every trip. The Army Corps of Engineers was created for the special purpose of monitoring changes in America's waterways, inspecting inspect rivers and continually maintaining any levees.

Life changes continuously. Who would have thought that one day we would be forced to wear a mask in public? As unexpected as the pandemic of Covid-19 occurred, life will always throw surprises your way. Sometimes change affects just your life, other times, everyone's life is turned upside down. And, like the river pilots, you must adapt to life. You must brace for change and continuously re-chart your course to get your destination. As the world evolves and as you mature, so do your goals. You're still headed in the same general direction, but your path will be a squiggly one as you pivot and curve to adjust to a new landscape. You must continually reflect and revamp your goals as you gain new information about your path forward. It's not about just adjusting your goals, it is also about sticking with them even though the path may delay your arrival or that you experience a major crash along the way.

My journey as an entrepreneur reflects this. I thought that if I focused all my time into my business, I wouldn't have to work for anyone else anymore. This is my ultimate goal. However, my path to this end is always evolving. I have changed business models several times. I've become disgusted and disenchanted a thousand times. I've walked away one hundred times. I've gone through three websites. All of these disappointing moments have always brought me to a new place in my start-up journey. Each time, I expressed myself in a different way. I came up with better ideas and found better solutions to old problems. I'm still pressing forward in my quest to be a full-time business owner. Be Preppy may not even be the company that takes me there, but I know I'll be there.

You'll constantly have to re-work your life's plans. What you wanted before may not be what you want now. How you thought it was going to happen probably won't play out as you like. Adulting has a way of making you re-learn yourself and updating your map just as the riverboat pilots had to do on every leg of the journey. Expecting challenges and twists and turns in life helps you learn to adapt and become resilient. Resiliency makes you flexible so that won't break under additional pressure or force. I am dating myself, but every time I think about resilience, I think about the film, *Remember the Titans*. There's a scene where the coach is doing a call and response during practice.

> Coach Boone: What are you?
> Team: Mobile, agile, hostile!
> Coach Boone: What is pain?
> Team: French bread!
> Coach Boone: What is fatigue?
> Team: Army clothes!
> Coach Boone: Will you ever quit?
> Team: No! We want some mo', we want some mo', we want some mo'!

Anytime your life gets rocky and adulting hits you with all it's might, recite these lines to yourself.

Headwaters affect everything downstream.

Headwaters are the primary contributors to a river's flow, and they are the beginning of the river. A river can start from one major source or it can begin with the trickle from hundreds of small streams. No matter how it begins, the health of the headwaters is more important than the volume of the flow. What happens to headwaters affects everything downstream. In adulting, your mindset and your perspective in life are your headwaters.

Your mindset is your collective way of thinking and processing the world around you. It almost pre-determines the angles in which you see problems, how you handle failure, and the level of effort you give, which ultimately predicts the outcome of the situation. Your mindset is based on years of life experiences and is validated every single time you make a decision. For instance, if you have a negative mindset, you may go into a job with distrust. And, you will see your co-workers as nothing but shady. Why? Because your mindset automatically tainted your perception of your colleagues. You pre-programmed yourself to block out any goodwill that they may have shown you. The wrong mindset can cause you to see something that's not really there. And, because our vision provides information to help us make decisions, a faulty mindset can cause you to make bad decisions.

Your mindset is one of the few things you can control. Having a faulty mindset on top of the challenges of adulthood will make your life 100 times harder. Therefore, choosing the right one is crucial to how the rest of your life plays out. In research, there are two types of mindsets: there's a fixed mindset and there's a growth mindset. For the purpose of the book, I will call them the lake and the river mindset. Individuals with the lake mindset see challenges as impossible to overcome and something to avoid altogether. They also give up easily, put in minimal effort, and hate feedback, yielding very few results and limited progression. Who has time to be the same person you were when you were 18 years old? Remember: water in lakes remain stagnant and if you travel around a lake long enough you end up right where started. You would also describe lake people as haters, literally, as they are intimidated by the others' success. But, unfortunately, there are a lot of miserable adults with the lake mentality. People with a growth or river mindset, on the other hand, anticipate challenges and see failure as a necessity for self-improvement. Because of their perspective of challenges, they understand that maximum effort is needed to overcome them. River people seek out feedback because they want to prevent wasting time on repeating mistakes. Instead of hating on the success of others, they find inspiration in their triumphs.

In adulthood, there will never be a shortage of problems. You may think that when you reach a certain status, they'll go away. But, they won't. In the words of my favorite choir director after someone would tell him they didn't have their fees for the school play: "times are hard for the rich and the poor." Problems are just a part of life. The only thing you can control is how you handle the challenges of adulthood and how you prevent them from dulling your glow and killing your purpose.

Having the river mentality has prevented me from falling to pieces as my whole world started to crumble beneath me. To some, it looked like I had lost everything: my job, my savings, my retirement, and nearly my home. This all happened within two years. I had my time of despair, but I made sure I limited my time dwelling in those dark moments. But, instead of thinking of what I "lost," I focused on what I'd gained. Unemployment provided me with the opportunity to wake up every morning to God's alarm clock. I had an opportunity to live in the moment with my family and close friends without worrying about work or traffic. I was grateful to even have a career that afforded me a retirement fund to deplete. To have an opportunity to be in life's lazy river, where I just floated and drifted for two-years discovering my purpose and waiting for the next breeze to blow, is an amazing experience. I could have tried to swim upstream and take any old job. But, ultimately, I had no energy left to fight backwards, especially when my intuition was telling me that heart's desire was waiting to be fulfilled downstream. Following my instinct, I found my flow.

I think this book would be worthless if I didn't warn you of the challenges that lie ahead. And the value would plummet even more if I didn't give you any real advice on how to handle the trials of adulthood. While I may advise you on major areas in life, it is nearly impossible to give the advice to solve every problem that you may encounter. Because mindset is the precursor to everything that happens in life, helping others to adjust theirs has been both my life's work and research agenda. Changing my mentality from a "woe is me" lake outlook to the river mindset helped me to ground myself. I've learned to convert every challenge into an opportunity to grow. I've used the naturally occurring momentum in my life to carry me forward. I've loosened up a lot to enjoy the journey and maximize every moment in life. I've stopped wasting time complaining about life's constant irritations. I choose to have joy, and unconditional happiness.

My editor and friend told me that she got a zen vibe from this book. This is very ironic because the author, me, has a tendency to be very anxious and wound up at the core. Everything needed to look, sound, and be perfect, which kept me circling around the lake. But, once I switched my mindset and found my solace in a real relationship with God, I began to come unbound and free from the weight of the world. I didn't have to have it all figured out. I didn't need to be Perfect Patty. You saw what happened when Perfect Patty messed up in *Why Did I Get Married*. She spiraled out of control. The river mindset is not about throwing caution to the wind and being irresponsible. It's about gaining strategic control of your life. It's about anchoring yourself your purpose, your mission, your priorities, and your values and letting go of anything that weighs you down. It's about moving forward whether you are holding on a piece of debris, floating on a life raft, riding on a tugboat, or cruising on a ship.

The hardest part about entering real adulthood is not having the faintest idea about what was going on. I had no anchor. No legitimate warnings about what lay ahead. No orientation class. No simulators. No test to take to see if I was ready. I wished my 22-year-old self would have had someone to give me a clue. What I needed was a strategy I could use in 99% of the situations I encountered. I didn't necessarily want hand holding, just some foundational advice. So, to you and my 20-something self, find your glow, identify your flow, and just go.

TO LIVE OR TO EXIST?

Live Wiser

TO LIVE OR TO EXIST?

You remember when you were told to wait as a kid? Whether it was waiting for a time-out to end, waiting for dinner to be ready, or waiting for your mom to finish shopping, or waiting for class to be over, it was as if time stood still. Everything took forever. A minute felt like an hour, and an hour felt like eternity. The older you get, though, time speeds up exponentially. One day, it's Monday and then "poof," it's Monday again. An adult year goes by in a blink of an eye. If you are not careful, four years of your life will pass and you'll still be in the same place as you were. You can't articulate any improvements you've made or any significant strides toward your goals. Adulting has a way of making you forget yourself. It will make you forget the sole reason you went to college and complete your degree. Remember the excitement you had when you first entered college. You had big dreams for the "good life". And, you began to chase them with zeal. In the words of Sugar Ray to Quick from the movie *Harlem Nights*: "... you're young and full of vigor and life."

As we age, that vigor slowly dissipates, and the zeal we possess slowly leaves. The disappearance of these youthful qualities has nothing to do with aging physically, but it has everything to do with how we face the challenges of life and adulting. The common struggles of life and disappointment we experience can slowly erode the hope we have to achieve the dreams and goals we set for ourselves. We often let the monotonous grind of a 9-5 wear us down until the only thing we look forward to is rushing home from work to sit pantless in front of the TV and escape our reality. Our dreams take a back seat to paying bills and working. We begin to forget them. *That's* how time slips away and that's how our youthful zeal disappears. It's as if our internal GPS loses connection and no longer provides us with directions toward our true north. Though you feel like you're moving, you realize that you are moving in circles and simply just existing in life.

This was supposed to be a straightforward, technical chapter on goal setting. However, I realized that goal-setting is the easy part. It's actually protecting those goals and keeping the youthful vigor needed to chase them freely is the hard part. You must learn how to manage your own goals, and, then you must learn how to adult-proof them. Yes, just as you would prep your house by covering sharp corners and dangerous electrical outlets before a baby arrives, you must protect your dreams and goals from debilitating disappointments and paralyzing fear. Insulating your goals helps you not to become an old, surly, bitter, and fearful adult who has been wandering in aimlessly in a life they've settled for. These adults don't have the right levels of emotional intelligence to be around people. I don't want you to become this person. I want you to be able to recognize the symptoms of just existing and prevent it before its onset. Many people don't even realize that they are just existing because they have daily justified contentment for mediocrity. You've encountered people like this. They laugh at your ambitions, telling you that you shouldn't want "all that", or that you are "doing too much", or that you should wait until your turn. They are Debbie-downers and will discourage you at every opportunity. They give you this advice from their own experiences of not accomplishing their goals. Don't listen! They are not the people to take advice from! It sounds wise because it comes from an experienced and seasoned individual, but it is dangerous. Even those who are very accomplished and successful, sometimes forget their origin. They forget their hustle and how they struggled to become who they are.

I can remember two noticeably clear instances where someone I admired gave advice that put a damper on my goals. One time when I didn't know any better and one time when I was just a little wiser. Needless to say, I experienced two different outcomes. The first was early on during my early professional career when I was about 23 or 24. Always the ambitious one, I had in my head that I wanted to retire at 35 from full-time professional employment and work for myself. However, when I casually mentioned this to a colleague, she said, laughing, "Oh, girl! That's just wishful thinking. We all want that." While it was a minute conversation, all I needed was just a minute of negativity to forget about that dream, which was uncommon but totally possible. That was nearly 12 years ago. Had I developed an aggressive savings goal and worked a little harder to bring in residual income, I would have been close to my dream. Maybe not retire at 35, but maybe 40 or 45, which is still a phenomenal feat. Nevertheless, I learned my lesson and I am reminded of it every time I read *Forbes* or any money magazine where I see a 30-something retire because they made significant moves when they were younger to increase their retirement portfolio and net worth.

Nearly 10 years later, I met an esteemed sorority sister that I had been wanting to meet for a long time. I admired her career path and wanted to gain some advice as I was in a career transition at the time. The conversation was going along well until I mentioned that I wanted to build up my consulting practice instead of going to work for someone else. She was actually a consultant and doing what I wanted to do. *Enter side eye emoji*. She said, "Oh, no. You don't want to do that. It's such a hassle dealing with paying your own taxes and health insurance." Again, I had my life planned out. I wanted to retire early. And, above all, I wanted to work full-time for myself. Becoming a higher education consultant had been one of my five-year goals at the time. I've always understood the tradeoff of being self-employed and taxes and health insurance was one of them. I hated being chained to a desk and fixed schedule. I would gladly trade the 9-5 for entrepreneurship if that was my only concern. I knew better. I actually understood where her advice was coming from. I know she was recently in an unfortunate public career transition herself and that she was trying to spare me from unwanted suffering. I graciously received her advice and thanked her for her time. Yet, I choose not to take it. In fact, not long after that conversation, I ended up with three consulting contracts from three universities. Yes, paying taxes was b!+@h, but I was in love with my work. This experience validated for me not to let anybody talk me out of my goals no matter how wacky they are. In fact, I only have a few friends with whom I share my plans, because I know they will hold my hand as I jump.

I have seen so many seasoned adults just sit and exist in reality and lose their fight for their dreams. They just exert just enough energy to maintain. Let me be clear, existing has nothing to do with the amount of money you make or wealth you have. You can exist in a big house, with a nice career, and full checking and savings account. Existing means you are going along with the status quo, not living on purpose, not growing and not evolving. You're alive, but you aren't living. This was exactly the way I felt after getting my PhD. I was just going to work, going home, and going to church. I wasn't happy in my situation at work, in my finances, and in life in general. I had stopped applying for jobs, cut out things to make ends meet. This meant no cable, no name brand cell company, no happy hours, no shopping, no Sunday brunches. I just began to cave in on myself. I was too tired to focus on my goals. It just felt like every time I did, I realized I couldn't even afford to dream. I had accepted that I was just going to remain at my job forever and make the best of it. I mean I did have a house and my car was paid for. Who was I to complain? I got comfortable and content with what I had. But, I missed out on so much time. You know, if I had pushed through with my idea for a company, I would now be in prime position to have real investors, perhaps be in a position to sell and put the cash in my retirement fund!? (Yes, I am still salty about the possibility of working longer than I wanted.) If I had not become so complacent with my job, I would not have had to defend my lack of years of management experience. I should have pushed a little harder to get another position offering me that experience. Just existing is actually more exhausting than just pushing through our comfort zones and fighting for what we truly want.

During the creation of this chapter, I stumbled upon my full Facebook profile. I don't know if you did this: but, as the one of the first few thousands of students on Facebook, we actually used our Facebook profile as a window into our lives. Now all we do is scroll the timelines and most everyone's profile is blocked now. I haven't felt a need to update it, seemingly, since 2008. There's no date to let me know that but, it's the quotes on my page that let me know exactly what year it was. One quote that stood out was from a famous hip- hop philosopher, Dwayne "Lil Wayne" Carter. It was from his 2008 work of art, *Tha Carter III*. It was the soundtrack of my summer and fall. *Reflects and smiles* That year had some good times and that album underscored them all. So, it makes sense that my quotes would feature Lil Wayne. I won't leave you to guess my favorite line. It's from the track, "Comfortable," featuring Babyface:

"Love. Live Life. Proceed. Progress." This line actually pairs well with another rap inspired mantra of mine, from the King of Petty, Curtis Jackson, aka 50 Cent: "Who said progress was a slow process?" In Wayne's song, he was talking to a woman about taking their relationship for granted by getting too comfortable and not putting in the effort. Just like in a relationship, you can't just check out of life when things go wrong. And you can't just do the bare minimum just to hold on to the good times and never seek anything better. You have to move and specifically move forward. That one line: "Love. Live Life. Proceed. Progress." is really what my life boils down to. I want to love genuinely even though there's a risk of me being hurt. I want to actually experience life and not just watch from the sidelines. I am always focused on persistence and consistency so that I am in a forward motion no matter if I am moving at one mile per hour or 100 miles per hour. It's taken me awhile to get this point and I have to remind myself daily of my commitment to consistent progress. Here's how I live progressively and prevent myself from falling into a habitual existence.

Be Intentional

Intent is so important that even our unjust criminal system takes it into account even though an act wasn't fully carried out. There was even a whole television show dedicated to just the thought and prerequisite action--*Law & Order: Criminal Intent* (Didn't watch it, as I'm loyal to Ice-T and Olivia Benson. And, yes, I know that's not his character's name.). Intent is a prerequisite for action. Before your body can do anything, your brain must make a deliberate choice to move, to blink, and breathe. You must make sure you are living every moment with intent. Goals don't just appear out of thin air. You actually have to choose to set a goal. This is where so many adults get stuck. In the busy pace of everyday life, we have a million wishes and a thousand mini-dreams. While some of our thoughts are wishful thinking--things that probably won't happen. You know, Jill Scott probably won't ever be my big sister and best friend because if I plan for that to happen, I would end up in jail for stalking. I am, however, still holding out for Erykah Badu to be my doula. (I have a real marketing strategy to make that happen.) These things probably will never come to pass, but there are some realistic goals that run rampant in our minds that we just dismiss as crazy thinking. Once we dismiss it as crazy thinking, we simultaneously throw away our intent. Thus, giving up on our goals. To turn our dreams into reality we must truly believe that it is possible. That belief, that intent, pushes us to act. Once we are intentional, we can turn an invisible thought into something of substance, so you can see it and act upon it.

How do you know if you are living intentionally? First, you are aware of your purpose and you align it with your actions and effort. You should be able to see this, or you should be able to present proof. For instance, when I was an advisor for a pre-med program at a university, I stressed to students that if I can't look at your calendar's to-do list and see your ambitions for a medical career, I won't believe you. I can tell if a student is serious about getting into medical school by what they tell me they did in a week and their summer plans. If I didn't hear that they studied for the MCAT, went to a study group, completed volunteer hours as a scribe, and filled out a summer program application, I would initiate a conversation to help them discover their true desire to be a doctor. If I heard them whining about how much time they spend studying for classes or lack of engagement from their professor, I would question their expectations.

The same goes for adults who say they want to start a business, buy a house, or save money. If I don't hear or see effort aligned with their goals, then I question their intentions. Why? Because beliefs should spur actions. This means that something is not quite right in their belief system. It could mean that there's doubt or fear. It also could mean that they are full of sh!t and just want to say something just to be part of conversations with people who are really doing things. Don't be one of those people.

Another sign of intentional living is that you take advantage of every moment. Just like Lil Wayne telling his woman not to take his love for granted, you should not take life for granted, not even a second. Make sure that every minute is used wisely. Am I saying run yourself into the ground? Nope, I am saying that you should be able to account for your time. I know we all have times where we spend the last five, ten, twenty, or thirty minutes of work looking at the clock, waiting for it to be exactly time to go home. Like we purposely just let the clock run out doing nothing. Unfortunately, we often do this in life. We don't strategically use our time wisely. There isn't a rhyme or reason to your day and when you think back, you can't recall what you did that day. You had no plans for yourself that day except going to work and coming home. You didn't set any expectations for yourself.

This isn't intentional living.

People who are intentional start their day with goals in mind. They track their time and constantly reflect on their progress. Think about this, everyone has 24 hours in their day. The difference for high impact individuals is that they maximize all 24 hours. Some people are amazed at many things I juggle and ask me how I have time for all of it. I have learned how to become laser focused on my purpose and align my priorities accordingly. Every moment of my life has a purpose where I rarely can say I have free time. My free time is already dedicated to one of my priorities, whether it is self-care, physical wellness, or spiritual upkeep. If I say I am doing nothing, then that means I am doing nothing on purpose, which means I am busy—doing nothing. This doesn't mean, though that I am so busy that I neglect my family and friends. Quite the opposite, I strategically make time for the people I prioritize and who prioritize me. I allot time to cultivate my relationships. And, if an urgent need arises, I only have a hand full of people that I would drop everything for. I have become proficient in controlling my time and not letting time control me.

While it's neither for the faint at heart, nor is it a perfect system, it has been one of the practices to which I owe my productivity and success. I've also realized that mastering time goes hand and hand with leadership and recurring success. I've unfortunately had to witness a supervisor, a senior administrator, learn this the hard way. She was seasoned but couldn't quite grasp this concept of control of time and leadership. She often let everyone dictate her schedule, including her boss. She found herself behind and overwhelmed. She stifled my productivity because she never had time to provide feedback or sign-off on my reports. She was always putting out fires and never planning ahead to prevent them. It was a sad situation. Her boss lost confidence in her because he could not see any progress. If I could go back in time and get the courage to tell her anything, it would be to break the cycle and stop letting people control your time. Your boss will respect you more if you said that you are unavailable. Limit the time faculty members can come into your office to complain. Send someone else to meetings that waste your time. Schedule time to think, to eat, to plan, and to do paperwork. Guard your schedule. Decline meetings. Set and explicitly communicate your boundaries. This is what I would tell her because this is how I functioned as a junior leader with 25 staff members.

And, guess what? We got a lot of things accomplished as a unit. Being nice nasty with my time helped me to garner respect from my team. I had more time for them when I set my boundaries and communicated them. It was simple. If my door is closed, I'm really busy. If it is not, you are welcome to enter. I actually had on my calendar open door time as well as time to walk and visit them in their offices. This is exactly what I would tell you. Be in control of the precious twenty-four hours God provides us every day.

In addition to controlling my time, I constantly monitor my behavior and my productivity. If I find that

I am spending too much time on tasks that align with my priorities, I have to discipline myself to cut things back. For instance, I love media, movies, and music. At the top of the year, I set some learning goals for myself. I noticed that I had barely made any progress in that area. But once I reflected on where my time went and identified my accomplishments, I realized that I've finished more movies and series on Netflix than I had books and podcasts on my lists. So, I made a deal with myself that if I must look or listen to something for entertainment at something, then it must be aligned to my personal learning goals. I want you to take two things from here: One, I made deliberate choices, and two, I had to adjust my behavior. Both of these actions are critical elements of living an intentional life. I've also observed myself and found that when I don't set my intentions it usually means that I won't do it. For example, when I actually tell myself the night before that I am going to work out in the morning AND layout my workout clothes, AND choose my workout, I actually do workout. When neither of those things happen, no exercise occurs.

Another hallmark of living an intentional life is the ability to articulate and execute a plan of action for any type of goal. I'm the friend that hears your ideas and says "okay, how can you make this happen"? It's that simple. This Think-Attack-Do nature arose from my paralyzing perfectionism procrastination habits. Everyone has a form of procrastination. Mine stems from my overthinking situations and tendency to play out a hundred scenarios before anything even takes place. I would convince myself that this idea is too complex to deal with now, so I'll deal with it later as if it would get simpler over time. I did this with regular chores, and I did this with dreams and ideas for my business. My first book could have come out years earlier, but I told myself I was not accomplished enough to write a book and I should wait until I was successful. I waited to launch my productivity company until I felt like I was proficient at productivity. I put off creating my non-profit because it seemed like something I should do when I'm older or when I had a nine-month tenured track position. I waited to launch my podcast until...well, I can't even remember why I put it off. I'm pretty sure it was a lame excuse about what I didn't have.

Once I started exploring the rise and fall of startups, I realized that many of the companies and services we can't live without (Instagram, Uber, and AirBnB) started with just an idea that was sketched out and put into action. I also learned about and embodied the concept of Minimum Viable Products or MVP. It was a concept in which startups used to test an idea without wasting time, money, and effort. So instead of putting all your time in the beginning to create an elaborate product, you would create a simple version that represents the core of your idea and build layer by layer from feedback from customers. Uber didn't start with a million cars on the highway. They began with one city, some customers, and some drivers to see if anybody truly wanted this service. If it had failed, no biggie. There weren't millions of dollars wasted, and if it succeeded, the next steps would be to make it better a little at a time. I began to apply this concept to not only my entrepreneurial perspective, but also my life. I just began to think about how to pare down my ideas so that they are not so big and scary that it would just cause me to push it into the recesses of my mind and abandon them. It also helps that I have a science background which causes me to see my whole life as an experiment.

Not until I connected entrepreneurship to science did it really click in my mind that this is how the Steve Jobs and Oprahs of the world think. In fact, seeing Oprah behind the scenes of building a new network encouraged me immensely. Here is this giant of a woman who could have remained successful in a lane she was comfortable in, but who decided to take a risk and try something new. She only really had one original show when she first started the network, but season by season, OWN grew. Same thing with Diddy and Revolt. If they can be comfortable with taking on new ideas and with the idea of calculated failure, then so can I. With that revelation, I taught myself to see the simplicity of ideas and the ease of execution to appoint where I am telling the governing board of my current employer that, "you know, the thought of raising a million dollars doesn't intimidate me." I see five, $200,000 gifts and in order to get five gifts I need to pitch to at least 20 people. That's now how my mind works. Nothing is off limits. No dream is too crazy or too big. All success has an infancy.

There is no overnight success. It evolves hour after hour, and day after day of small wins.

I think most people, including myself, can get caught in the next time or the right time. The question to myself is why? Why not now? It doesn't mean just because you start now that it will manifest immediately. You have to start something and give it time to grow. They underestimate the real time it takes for success to happen. But at the same time, we also overestimate what it takes for success to happen. The only way to know for sure is to create a well-informed plan and set goals. Once you see it on paper, then you can estimate the time it may take and set your expectation accordingly.

This is something that I am working on daily. I sit and stare at a pile of clothes and say I don't have time to do laundry, but sitting, staring, and thinking about my laundry took more time than actually putting the clothes in the machine. Likewise, I have to constantly talk myself out of delaying bigger actions, like buying properties or investing. I can still plan efficiently now to buy another house although my situation may not be ideal for me. There are still things I can do now to set myself up for success. I can stash away cash for saving, which will take a long time. I can save more when I have more, but now I am saving what I can. I can still look for properties, educate myself, and narrow down real estate agents I may want to work with later. I am executing this part of my plan now, knowing that I may not see the results until later. However, it will manifest sooner than if I wait to plan and execute later. In short, there's no harm in planning. The harmful part is never planning at all and not setting real intentions because you are waiting for the right time or making excuses for your fear.

What does a well-intentioned and well position plan of action look like? It is specific, measurable, achievable, relevant, and timely or SMART. The Bible says write the vision and make it plain. An intentional plan of action requires detailed goals, objectives, and tactics that embody all levels of details that will answer who, what, when, where and why. In my book, (Ha! This is my book.) vague, nondescript goals are simply wishes and wishes are for a fantasy world.

First and foremost, your goals have to be specific. I want to be rich is a common wish. I want to have

$50k in cash, $500,000k in my retirement portfolio, a 10% debt ratio, and $1 million dollars in assets is a very specific goal. See the difference. I used to say I wanted a good job. Well, what is a good job? After a beautifully, tragic experience (you'll learn about that in the next chapter on careers) I've learned to make sure I am very specific in my career goals. Instead of saying I want a good boss, I say that I want to collaborate with a transformational leader who has optimal levels of emotional intelligence and understands the importance of leading holistically with a humanist perspective. That's an example of a specific goal. Goal setting and productivity is my niche. But, guess what? I still suffer from general-itis. Last year was my first time ever setting a profit target in my 10 years of being an entrepreneur. Seeing it on paper over and over again, fuels my fire to get to the money.

So, how will I know when I've "gotten to the money"? Great question. The answer to that question lies in the measurable quality of the goal. It simply answers the question of, "how will I know that I have achieved the goal?" You should always create your own measuring stick. This goes back to our discussion on social comparison. You can't measure your goals by someone else's ruler. You can use their success to see what's possible, but in the end, you have set and live by your own standards of achievement. So, in setting my profit targets for the first time, I had to write down the amount of money that I wanted to have by the end of the year.

In making this decision, I could have used the standard some of my good friends make in their prospective businesses, but we weren't in the same industries. Also, I know I wasn't putting in the work like they have, so I could set a goal that I wanted to make $100k in nine months, but it would be totally unreasonable. It was not achievable. In setting SMART goals, there is an optimal place to be where you aren't scared to be ambitious and you are a little bit of a realist. Yes, I could have made up my mind that I wanted to make 100k in nine months, but realistically, it wasn't going to happen for a variety of factors. It is totally possible to do 10k because I reached those levels previously.

Don't set yourself up for failure and disappointment by setting goals based on false ideas or misinformation. This is what makes goals both achievable and relevant. Make sure you do your homework in determining what's possible and what it takes for it to happen. I have long admired my friend who does really well as a negotiation coach. She gave me a sneak peek at the behind the scenes work to gain her success, and I was blown away. She really puts in the work and she's made a ton of sacrifices that most people wouldn't make in the hustle for success.

A lot of the people you see from afar are doing well, but make sure you learn about how they achieved what they did. And, there's nothing special about you that makes you exempt from the work needed for success. In my academic coaching days, students were heartbroken all the time when they failed exams. I ask them how they prepared. The response was always, "I studied hard last week." On the verge of quitting, because they thought they did everything humanly possible to pass, I would share with them what the top students did to prepare. Amazingly, the majority of students just think top grades come easily. When I tell them that the average student with a 3.5 average or more, previews material before they come to class, studies everyday including the weekends, goes to tutoring, visits office hours which totals to about 20 hours a week outside of class they are blown away. They realized the work it took to just "be smart." As you set achievable goals, factor in the work that it takes and the work you are willing to put in at a given time, which brings us to the "T" in SMART.

Time is the defining factor between a wish and a goal. A wish pairs well with someday. I'm going to buy a house someday. When there is no time associated with a goal, there will be no need for action. There's no urgency, no deadline, and nothing that will cause you to spring into action. There is no association on a calendar. There is a day of week called someday. This means you really have no intention of doing anything at all. To be intentional, you have to connect your goals to a date or specific time. Your goals must be time-bound. Even if you don't make your deadline, at least you can measure your progress and set a new date.

Also, make sure you are able to toggle back and forth between your long-term and your short-term goals to ensure their alignment. Ten adult years goes by so fast that it can almost be considered short-term.

In thinking through your goals, you always want to work backwards. If you know you want a certain amount of assets later in your life or be at a certain place in your career, you need to break the long-term goal down into smaller milestones and incorporate those milestones into your short-term goal plans. Continue breaking down your short-term goals into yearly, quarterly, monthly and weekly goals. The continual reflection on the future combined with the consistent monitoring of the presents helps you to live with both intent and hope.

    Living intentionally is key to preventing your fall into habitual existence. Being intentional begins with a thought that will propel you into action. That first action must be the creation of solid, executable, SMART goals. Those goals then break down into strategies and tasks that you will use to take command of your day. The commitment to those goals will push you continually to be aware of how you are spending your time. Your goals then become your internal GPS that will continue to advance you forward.

Be Resilient

Another way to prevent habitual existence is to build your resilience. If you Google "resilience," you'll find it defined as the capacity to recover quickly from difficulties; toughness or the ability of a substance or object to spring back into shape; elasticity. To become resilient, you have up your "snap-back factor." When most people say you need to stay strong, you think of hard things like diamonds. Diamonds are known for strength. They are made under pressure, but if you apply too much force, diamonds will break, and they can't be put back together. There will be difficulties in life... you can bet on it. The only thing you can control is how you respond. Are you going to fall into a million pieces at even the shadow of a challenge? Or, are you going to confront it head on, process your experience, and pivot accordingly? Not being able to snap back causes you to become lost and discombobulated. You forget who you are and where you are headed. So, you stay in this time loop of replaying out the hard times, reliving the experience, and throwing a pity party. You began to use every failure and barrier as an excuse to not move forward, falling into habitual existence.

Increasing your snap-back factor starts by recognizing the cause of life's challenges. I learned from my pastors that challenges happen because of human error on your part, human error from others, or just by inherent randomness of life. Stuff happens. You make mistakes. And, no one is perfect. Once I internalized this, my snap-back factor increased exponentially. Now, my first step is to ask myself, "did I mess this up?" If there is a clear answer, I tell myself to do better and to take the "L" and move on. If someone else is at fault, I try to get the situation rectified. If it can't be rectified, then I choose to forgive, move on, and adjust accordingly. If it's just a part of life, I don't take it personally. I adapt accordingly.

Another way to increase your snapback factor is to constantly remind yourself of a time when you overcame something really difficult. Our mind has a way of tricking us into forgetting our previous successes. We block out the times we fought, hustled, and grinded our way out of a tough spot. We forget that we've won. Even the times that we lost weren't so bad, because in the end we survived. I always remind myself of the challenges I conquered in the past and how much stronger I am now to fight the battles ahead. And, when all seems lost and I think that this one thing will be the end of everything, I just breathe.

Over the years, after being more empathetic and sensitive to others' situations, I began to realize that waking up day after day in a bed under a roof with my health intact is proof that I have a chance to make things right, to make things better. When I begin to be dramatic and have an adult tantrum when things go wrong, I always think of a line from *Hangover II* and a viral meme that my friends love to use, "But, did you die?" This was Mr. Chow's response to Phil's complaints about "just being shot" when Mr. Chow had just been resuscitated. When your goals aren't going as planned and it seems there are little fires everywhere in your life, you have to take a breath and realize that you have everything you need: life. People have gone through actual life and death situations and were able to bounce back with grace and joy. This should give you the confidence not to let life break you. You may have to bend and contort yourself uncomfortably, but you don't have to break apart.

During my time of consulting and exploring (unemployment), I was facing foreclosure and bankruptcy. My home was flooded and less than a year later, I lost my job. A lot of people were concerned for me. There were times I was concerned for myself. There were a few days where I absolutely had no money. Not like fake broke, but real broke. I would be lying if I said I was jolly 100%, of the time, but I would say that at least 95%, I was happy and content. I didn't stop chasing my goals because I lost a job, or I was losing my house, or that I would be in financial ruin. Leaned into them more. I threw myself into things that didn't require any money: being creative. I wrote my first book. I created a podcast. I worked on my business plans. But, most of all, I practiced gratitude every minute of the day. Every bite that ate, every moment I laid in my bed, every mile I drove, I thanked God for it. Let's be honest, there are a lot of homeless people who had everything taken away for one reason or another and didn't have family to take them in. I could have easily been homeless. My parents could absolutely have used their rights to say that I was too grown to move back home. But they didn't. I was extremely grateful to have parents who were young, able, and alive to even help me through my rough times. They didn't make me help with the bills. They didn't force me to get a job. They supported me through it all. Many people don't have that option, and I didn't want to take that for granted. I chose not to let this time break me. I chose to pretend like I was in *The Matrix,* spiritually trained to duck and dodge all the things aimed at me. After that period of my life, I felt the strongest I've ever felt. I know that I can handle anything. And now that I'm writing during a pandemic, I'm even calmer. I'm counting different blessings and preparing to take on new challenges. I'm still weathering the consequences of not working for a year and a half, but I don't have any regrets.

My snap-back quotient is at an all-time high now. I'm proud of myself. I used to be the dramatic fall-apart queen. If 21-year-old Erin experienced the last two years, she would have thought herself a failure. She would have made terrible mistakes out of desperation. She would have taken a random job just to say she had a job. She would have forgotten about all her goals and used her lack of money and imperfect timing as excuses not to take action. But 35-year-old Erin is a different woman. An adult woman.

There are just some things you are going to face and confront head on as you are getting on your feet financially, settling in as a new professional, and finding yourself. Use these moments early on to build your resilience, propel you towards your goals and out of habitual existence.

Focus on Continual Improvement and Growth

Lastly, the way to prevent habitual existence is to not only focus on achievement but also on getting better. I've seen a lot of this from living in a small town. People work so hard to get to a safe place in life (a comfortable place to live, a new car, and a stable job), they won't risk a hair on their head to go outside of their comfort zone. On the other hand, there are people who dream big and achieve their goals but are too busy polishing their accomplishments to do anything new. Once you have achieved everything on your list, set new goals. There's always room for improvements and growth. There are always new levels to reach. As the world evolves, the opportunities to explore drastically increase. And, we are living longer than previous generations. You have time to keep dreaming, executing, and re-imagining your life over and over again.

A major part of continual improvement is reflection. It's a part of that self-awareness we talked about in "Grown-Up Glow-Up". You should consistently spend time assessing your life from different angles. Plot out your next moves to capitalize on your strengths. Improve your weaknesses. Satisfy your curiosities. Essentially, become a better human. Reflect not only on how to become better, but also to acknowledge and celebrate your progression. This is easier said than done. We get so wrapped up in our busy lives and so weighed down in our disappointments and feelings that we really don't want to do the deep work that comes with reflection. Circle back to intentionality. You have to set intentions to reflect and actually make real plans to do it. It looks different for everyone.

I admit I've let life get the best of me many times where I neglected myself and I didn't set aside time to gather myself. This all stopped in 2018. About one year into my time of unemployment, I had let too many people and things encroach on my time meant for me and only me. By December of 2018, I had become overwhelmed and tired. I didn't have enough money to take a full vacation, but I needed something. I scraped up enough money and loyalty points to do a staycation at a hotel in Baton Rouge. It was enough for me, as I was staying with my parents at the time in my hometown an hour away and so it felt like a getaway. I used that time to pray, meditate, relax, and think. I bought along markers and butcher paper that I hung on the walls. I had a separate sheet for each area of my life: me, my business, my non-profit, and my career. I brainstormed what I wanted to accomplish in the next 12-16 months. One area I had noticed about myself was that I would have great ideas, but I didn't execute them in a time that would allow maximum quality. This was unfortunate because though I was great at strategic planning for institutions and organizations, I didn't do this for myself. This little time that I took for myself to reflect helped me to progress significantly in 2019. I had to fight hard to do it and resist temptation to make excuses not to do it. You don't have to wait until a new year to take time out to reflect. You can set aside time each month, each week or each quarter to do this. All you need is a distraction free zone and a notebook to capture your thoughts.

The focus on continual improvement also helps you to get rid of the all or nothing mentality. You know that mindset that takes over when you don't have the career, the house, the car, the business, or the kids by 25. You have to pace yourself. Not all success comes in your youth or at one time or even when you want it to happen. You always have to mark your starting point and chart your movements to your ultimate goal. This will help you not fall apart at your failures and build resilience. And, as a recurring theme in this book, your starting point is different from everyone else's and so will be your rate of progression. There's a delicate balance in adulting between taking your time and not making excuses for putting it off until you're older. It *is* possible for you to hit your ambitious financial goals, but you must appreciate your progress towards that goal as well as be okay with not hitting your mark if it doesn't happen. Be bold and courageous in setting your goals but fall in love with the process and the progression of it and celebrate at each milestone.

From birth to 18, your life was pretty much planned out for you. From telling you when and what to eat to which schools to attend to what grades you were expected to make, your parents did most of the goal-setting for you (if you were fortunate). Maybe they cheered you on and motivated you at every turn. After you turned 18, they still had goals for you, but it was little they could do to help you achieve them. After college, they still have dreams for you. They want you to live better than they did. However, as an adult, you have to take the reins. There will be no one to push you better than you can yourself. There is no one who can see the vision for your life as clear as you. This is both the burden and the beauty of adulting. Adults who get caught in just existing and coasting through life are still needing someone to help them calibrate their internal GPS. You have to fight like hell not to fall into habitual existence. You must live intentionally, be resilient, and continually improve.

Love. Live life. Proceed. Progress.

CONFIDENTIAL CAREER COMMANDMENTS

Live Wiser

CONFIDENTIAL CAREER COMMANDMENTS

By now, you've read bits and pieces of my career story in the preceding chapters. You've probably ascertained that it's been a rocky journey. It has been. Still, what I've learned over the past few years is that I am definitely not an outlier when it comes to career disdain. No matter how much you love what you do or how much you love your job, working sucks. It sucks even worse when you fall into an American culture trap of tying your career to your identity. Apparently, other cultures find it odd that the first question Americans ask a stranger is, "What do you do for a living?" (I just learned that fact about two weeks before writing this chapter.) We ask that question like it's going to tell us everything we know about a person as if you meet a doctor or a lawyer you immediately make assumptions that they are very fine people doing very well for themselves. Our society has put so much emphasis on careers that we base our value and self-worth on how well our career is going. We even committed four to eight additional years of our life to make sure we have a solid career. When, in truth, our career is just a fraction of who we are as a person. That is the purpose of finding your *Ikigai* in the "Grown-Up Glow-Up". It was to help change your perspective on purpose and help you see that your career is tangent to your purpose, not central to it. It took me nearly ten years after college to place to realize that a career is only one minor piece to my puzzle.

In "Recalibrate Your Expectations," I explained that I thought that a career would be one in which I stayed at one or two jobs for a long time and which I would climb up the ladder relatively easily. That's what I saw with professionals in my community, and that's what I was taught in my career development classes. In today's world, a career is a series of jobs that one has over a lifetime. Just like this definition, all the things that I thought I knew about careers were challenged harshly by my reality. None of the career development or career planning workshops or classes prepared me for what professional life really was. It was like there was a secret curriculum that I didn't have access to. Yes, all the standard tips like how to dress professionally and how to apply are great. Yet, there were no lessons to help you when things go wrong.

I'm writing this book during the Coronavirus pandemic. I had a conversation with a good friend who just happens to be a career coach. I said I feel bad for the 2020 college graduates who had to enter the workforce on the brink of a recession. She kindly reminded me that they would be okay. I laughed out loud and said, "you're right." "We did graduate from college in a double dip recession." I graduated from undergrad in 2007 in the worst economy—especially in Louisiana. Our state had significant cuts to higher education. Guess what? I wanted to be a professor. Even by 2009 when I had my Master's, I couldn't even get an adjunct teaching position at the local community college. I was devastated. I had to rethink my career path at that point because the only way to gain a teaching position was through experience and the only way to get quality experience is through getting a teaching position. See the dilemma? There's not a lesson in any book about career pivoting in a recession. I had to learn on the fly. I'm sharing what I learned with you through my personal career commandments. But, before I do, let me take you through an abridged journey of my career.

My professional career started at a big state university as a STEM Learning Strategies Consultant in the learning center. This wasn't my first choice in starting my career. I was halfway finished with my PhD program and had just received my master's degree and was still working on my dissertation research. I didn't have any luck finding an instructor's level teaching position in Louisiana because of the cuts to Higher Education. Adjunct or part-time instructors were in the first way of layoffs. And, so all classes had to be taught by full-time tenured or tenured track positions. I began to look into other options that kept me in Higher Education and leveraged my science background. I found a position that happened to be connected to my dissertation topic. I applied and was selected. I stayed there for about four years. I took advantage of every opportunity I could. I was partly an academic coach to students and a consultant to faculty who gave strategies to improve course performance. I also trained tutors and worked on marketing strategies for the center. I helped to write grants with multiple departments. I sat on university diversity committees and various committees in our Student Affairs division. I stayed there for about four years until I was recruited to a small university in Kentucky.

In Kentucky, I was an Assistant Provost for Student Success. I was responsible for improving the program, processes, and policies that impacted student performance and in class as well as their progression and graduation rate. I worked with students, staff faculty, and other administrators to make this happen. I learned a lot about politics, and toxic work environments. We had turnovers at the President and Vice-President levels almost every six months. I eventually was "laid off" after the third President took office. I was there for a little more than two years.

This was the point in which I was happily unemployed for about another two years. I was then recruited to apply for an Executive Director position at a non-profit in New Orleans which focuses on improving college completion for low-come students. I am in this position as I write this book. I am responsible for strategic planning and growing the organization and everything that comes with being a chief executive officer.

So that's my summary of my professional career. I didn't include the various part-time jobs that I've held alongside my full-time positions. Yes, I'm a bit of a work-a-holic. Now that I've gotten you up to speed, let's delve into those career commandments.

Thou shalt look ahead.

A career is a series of jobs, not a random assortment of jobs. To prevent having a random assortment, you must be strategic in plotting out your series. If you have already begun the job search, you probably have found yourself frustrated with the job postings. If you haven't, prepare yourself. Nothing made me angrier than finding a great entry level position, requiring way more experience than a brand-new college graduate would have. Even worse, the pay would be insulting. I admit now that I didn't do as much research as I needed to at the beginning of my undergraduate degree. If I could do it over again, I would plan better. I was under the assumption that a PhD would be the only thing I needed to be a professor. So, when I changed my mind from completing a PhD in Biology to one in Science/Math Education, I thought I was fine. I thought since I could have a Master's in Biology and training in education, that I could do what I ultimately wanted to do: teach first-year biology and conduct research on effective teaching practices. Joke was on me.

When I finally did graduate with my PhD in Science/Math Education and began looking for tenured-track teaching positions in biology departments, I found that positions required what I didn't have. They required PhDs but they valued terminal degrees in hard sciences (biology, chemistry, math) and not the education versions. Even when I looked at positions in science education, they wanted experience in K-12 education, which I did not have. I was stuck and disgusted. I mean I don't regret switching from a biology PhD to Science/Math Education PhD. I know I wouldn't have been happy. I was disgusted at myself for not doing my research properly. I can't go back, but I can help you not make the same mistake.

My advice to you is take a backwards approach. We've been taught to take a job and then find wait until we want to leave, or we get laid off to find a new job. Or, we leave to get more money, which is not the healthiest perspective. This is a reactive method. The backwards approach is proactive and involves identifying an ultimate job or position and plotting out the experience you need to get that position. Your first position bridges the gap between the experience that qualifies you for the role and the experience you need to progress to your next position. You proceed from position to position until you are ready to qualify for your ultimate job.

I learned this backwards approach by trial and error, but this was reinforced during my experience at a leadership institute for women in higher education and by my career coach. At the institute, I learned to plot out how to become a college president by studying the qualifications of the role and seek ways to gain the experience along your current career path. I know I need development and fundraising experience as well as experience in being a chief executive officer. My current position leverages my experience as senior administrator and knowledge of college success while I am gaining development and leadership experience. My next position will build on the experience that I am currently gaining by either deepening my skill set or complimenting it.

My career strategy will be to look for opportunities that will allow me to lead large non-profit higher education-based organizations. My career coach shared a short-term strategy that fits in with this concept. He said that your search for your next job should start anywhere from nine months to a year before you want to transition from your current position. In that time, you should be spying out your next position, gaining the experience needed, and networking with people who could connect you to potential leads. No matter where if you are comfortable in your current position, you should always be prepared by knowing what is out there and keeping your resume updated.

Thou shalt keep an open mind.

One way to enhance your career search strategy is to keep an open mind. This involves considering a wide variety of settings, industries, and positions. I definitely had to do this with my biology background. Since I changed my mind about being benchtop scientist, I had to rethink my options. It seemed like every time I searched for jobs that required a science degree in Louisiana it had to do with being outside. And, for those who know me well I am allergic to everything that's outside (trees, bushes, grass, cats, long-haired dogs, etc....) I wasn't going to apply for those. So, I had to branch out past the biology degree requirement. I had to keep an open mind when I couldn't enter academia as a professor. So, I looked for jobs that were higher education related, that used my critical thinking skills I'd learn from my science courses and my experience in tutoring, mentoring and program planning. I searched for positions in student support, college access, and STEM recruitment. I looked at higher education institutions, tech corporations, and non-profits. At the time, I thought I was just desperate. But then as I gained real-world adulting and management experience, I realized that this was how career management worked.

There are so many companies and organizations that undertaking the world's most unique problems that require unique professionals to solve. There are so many different positions out there that need a combination of skills that go beyond just the degree requirements. You must learn how your degree can be applied across industries. Conduct strategic research on titles, job descriptions and requirements in different contexts. For instance, if you are a finance major you can look for comptrollers, assistant bursars, business analyst, and budget coordinator positions if you are looking in higher education. These positions may look different in medicine, in Hollywood or on Wall Street. The core skills are the same, but they vary in settings. And the example just highlights just a tiny sample of places you can work.

Millions of small businesses, non-profits, and government-based positions have available positions. The intersection of industries and unique missions of organizations create cool unique positions and careers. Who do you think help writers create those medical or crime dramas? Who creates the animations for cartoons or the illustrations in your textbooks? Who creates the Geico ads for TV or voices the actual Geico? There is a job for everyone, but it takes a little while to find your perfect match. What is the perfect match? It's a job that allows you to use your college acquired skills, your life derived skills, and your personality. It also aligns to your personal values. Sounds familiar? It all leads to back to your purpose and *Ikigai*.

Keeping an open mind is not only about industries and companies, but more so about not keeping YOU out of your own job search. You deserve to give yourself the opportunity to work in a place that meets your needs. It was important for me to interact with students. It was important for me to impact college success. It was important for me to improve STEM education. It was important for me to be creative and collaborative. But I like small intimate environments, so me working for a big education-based corporation would be a no-go even though it presents elements I desire.

So, when you are in the job search begin with searching for missions that speak to you, then look for ways to apply your skills. If you are an accountant, you may not be happy to work at a large firm if you hate capitalism and corporate greed. But you may be happy to crunch numbers for an organization that helps fight child hunger. Conversely, if you like competition, you may like working for a big sales department. You must constantly keep your purpose, values, and talents in mind when finding your career match. Now, when you are first starting out, you may not get a position that checks all your boxes. You may not be in a place to turn down positions; however, if you research and search correctly, you will have more jobs that have the qualifications you desire.

The other part of keeping an open mind is about your first job. My first job was a good position that allowed me to grow. Was it somewhere that I wanted to stay forever? No. Was I searching for other positions while I was there? Yes. The pros outweighed the cons, enabling me to pass on other offers or separate from the company all together. I kept an open mind about the position. I took advantage of all the opportunities I needed to enhance my resume for my next position. Therefore, you must look ahead and keep an open mind at the same time. My biggest mistake was neglecting to proactively manage my career. I waited until the last minute to make a career move instead of continuing to foster my career opportunities. Don't make this mistake. You have to both stay in the present to maximize your current opportunity and keep an open mind about your future strategy.

Thou shalt not be afraid to move.

Houston and DC. Those were the main two cities to which I was willing to move. That makes me giggle. I really have been trying to move to those places since 2012. I consistently searched for jobs in Texas and the DC-area in all my career phases and never really had a legit offer. During that period when I became frustrated with applying, location preferences became a non-factor for me. I just wanted out. So, when the call came inviting me to move and work in Kentucky, I said, "yes, please!" I was single with no kids. All I had was my house. It wasn't a bad drive from Louisiana just in case my family needed to get to me. I had nothing to lose. Many people, especially from my small hometown, asked me how I could move all the way to another state where I didn't know anyone. It was simple to me. I just packed up and moved. If I stopped to think for more than the few moments, I would have talked myself out of doing it. The job in Kentucky was a bittersweet experience, but I loved everything about moving away. It was freedom for me. I had lived near my family and friends all my life. I was feeling a little bit suffocated by my life, my obligations, the lack of opportunity. I just needed a change. I don't regret moving at all. Although my next move was back to home state, I wouldn't hesitate to move again, and I would encourage you to take the leap of faith too. Why?

Moving away and out of your comfort zone exponentially boosts your Grown-up Glow-up. It will strengthen your resilience and your problem-solving ability. Moving away forces you to rebuild your network, test your discernment, and recalibrate your spidey-senses. It will expand your cultural knowledge and your ability to connect with more people. Moving away expands your career possibilities by diversifying your resume and expanding your network. Do not be afraid to move.

I took the leap of faith. Some of my friends took the leap. But, some of my friends didn't. They just stood on the ledge and looked over. As a result, they were and still are frustrated with the number of job options by limits they've actually placed on themselves. The frustration is probably exacerbated by living in a region without a diverse economy. If you were to meet them and ask them why they did not move, they'll present a convincing argument. It could be that they didn't know anybody in the city. Their mate (not as in a spouse) couldn't find a job or didn't want to move with them. They didn't have any money to move. They couldn't move as a single mother without support. All of these are great arguments, but none of these are impossible to overcome nor outweigh the benefits of relocating if the job is worth it.

I'm not saying you always must say yes to moving. I've turned down positions in other states that weren't quite right. My charge to you is to heavily consider applying to a job or accepting the offer even if you must relocate. I will also challenge you to move away and gain experience while you don't have any responsibilities, if you can. That way, when it's time for you to plant yourself and settle down, you don't have any regrets. You won't have to have heavy conversations with your partner or have to really think about uprooting your kids. And even if you have to relocate with your family, it won't be such a shock to you, because you've done it before.

Also, keep an open mind about the locations. Don't be so quick to cross a job off the list because of you don't know anything about the place or it sounds boring. Remember every job and life change is for a purpose. You don't have to stay there forever. You just need to gain the experience, build your network and meet your personal career goals to progress to your next career stop. Now I am a country, suburban kind of girl. I need a car to get around, a driveway, and significant distance from my neighbor. But, if the opportunity checks off enough of my boxes, I won't hesitate to move and be a city girl for a minute. I know I need that experience to help me evolve, because I am set in my ways.

I am naturally an anxious person. So, my default setting is usually set to no and what if. I was in a precarious position in which my default was overridden by my desperation. I am so glad that I overcame my internal dialog and moved away. Don't let fear, a few obstacles or discomfort keep you from expanding your career horizons and ultimately living the life you want to live.

Thou shalt negotiate.

"I am calling to formally offer you the position." Those are the magic words you cannot wait to hear. But don't get so excited that you give an immediate yes. You should be excited, but you should also negotiate your offer. I didn't quite understand this concept when I accepted my first professional position after college. I didn't have a chance to counter the offer because it was countered for me. They offered me more than what the position announcement stated mainly because they already knew the salary was low for my qualifications. That doesn't happen often. I did, however, stumble through conversations to reach a compromise on my start date and temporary part-time status. That was the extent of negotiations. Compensation negotiations were not a part of my career education. I was never encouraged to speak up and ask for what I needed. I felt like I should be just satisfied with what they give me and if they wanted me to have more that would give it. Sounds right, huh? Nope! It is the hiring managers job to hire the best person at the lowest end of the salary range.

I really didn't get hip to the negotiation thing until my one of good friends began her career coaching business and began to specialize in negotiations. She always posted stats on social media of the differences in salary for men and women of different races. As a minority and a woman, I was already dispositioned to receive a lower salary. Discrimination could partially be to blame, but research shows that women lack the knowledge and confidence to initiate salary negotiations. Men tend naturally ask for exactly what they want despite of self-evaluated qualifications. Later in my work to improve employability for underserved college students, I learned that minority, first-generation and low-income graduates have income disparities even after graduation. That fact hit home as well as a first-generation college student. My parents definitely didn't teach me about negotiations strategies. I mean they encouraged me to apply for jobs that I didn't feel qualified for, but their post-offer advice was non-existent. It's only natural as they worked the same job for more than 20 years. So that's why negotiation is a career commandment. I want to be the one person who challenges you to do this if no one will. Making sure you maximize your first starting salary as it sets the tone for the rest of your career. Those who negotiate earn more throughout their lifetime.

Negotiation, just like listening, is a skill. I am extremely fortunate to have a friend who is a top negotiation coach. If she would let me, I would pay her in gold. I used her to coach me through two negotiations. And the things she told me to ask for I would have never thought to included. The biggest thing that I learned is that negotiation doesn't have to be just salary. In many cases entry level positions have a small range, so salary discussions may be limited. However, you should consider asking for professional development allowances, annual raises, technology provisions, travel allowances, increase in time off, flex scheduling, and work from home days.

Always remind yourself that it doesn't hurt to ask. They will not think you are being demanding. No one is going to look out for your best interest except for you. You should always know your worth. Resolve to do this even if you feel like you do not have the experience, or you aren't qualified enough. It takes practice to build up confidence to negotiate. So, starting at the beginning of your career makes the most sense. Don't wait like me until you get the "big job" and you're terrified to speak up for yourself. But don't take my word for it. Read Jacqueline Twillie's *Don't Leave Money on the Table* and thank me later.

Dr. Erin Wheeler

Thou shalt be clear about your non-negotiables.

What you want in a job is not the mirror opposite of what you don't want. Knowing what you don't want is something that takes time and experience. Your first position will be by trial and error. If you are observant and aware, you'll get wiser after each job experience. There are preferences that are more imaginative than realistic in which you know you'll never find in any job situation and that it is not a make or break situation in which you'll turn down an offer. There are other preferences that you feel strongly about, but if they are paired with other desirables you would overlook not having it. Then there are your non-negotiables. These are things that would absolutely make you say no to a job even if the job was presented on a silver platter. A non-negotiable is something that is not up for discussion or modification.

Non-negotiables are not always about money. I can be anything that goes against your values, threaten your mental and emotional health, or make it impossible for you to succeed. My list of non-negotiables started before accepting my second professional position. It was my first leadership role, and I knew I need certain guarantees for me to have the highest potential for me to succeed. I wouldn't have taken the job if I was going to be micromanaged and had my creativity stifled. I wouldn't have taken the job if I wasn't allowed to be innovative or allowed to fail without explanation. And, I wouldn't have taken the job if there was not a realistic budget or access to resources in order to do my job. Those were the first items on the non-negotiables list. After that job came to an end and I began to search again, my list expanded.

One non-negotiable that was placed at the top, was a toxic work environment. I need an environment that doesn't foster competition and replaces pettiness with collaboration and empathy. Because everyone has on their best face at an interview, it is hard to decipher the what's real and what's not. You have to really research the company, speak with other employees, ask the right questions during the interview, and be observant of interactions between colleagues.

My time in leadership in higher education was bittersweet, but it taught me a lot about the impact of leadership on the work environment and productivity. I technically had two types of work environments I would navigate. The first was senior leadership, faculty and staff. These interactions were fraught with fear, insecurity, selfishness, power, and greed. I found myself on guard at every email, conversation, or meeting. It was like the *Game of Thrones* meets *The Wire*. I was so green and honest that I was sincere in every situation. My focus was on the students. I did not have any intention to embarrass anyone or make myself seem better. However, everyone was so easily offended that it was like walking on land mines. A simple question or request from a colleague would transform into a huge argument or even a dismissal. If they weren't offended, they always had an ulterior motive or different agenda that was absolutely not about serving students. I didn't realize what an emotional toll it took on me and everyone around me. Staff turnover was high. I was exhausted by 10 AM every day. I hated to get out of bed to face the day because I knew it would just be filled with BS. I adapted the best I could and found ways to spend more time in my office that I had secured. I had a staff of 22 that were distributed across a few departments. Those offices that I could pull together and put in one spot were moved to the same hallway as my office. I created a safe, tucked-way space for myself and the employees that I managed. I created for them what I wished I had with my own colleagues and supervisors. I tried to make sure everyone was working together as a team and no one had to compete. I tried to foster a sense of authenticity in that everyone could be themselves and empathy so that we led with care and compassion for each other. I tried to make sure I spent as much time as I could with my staff because that was the only time I felt at peace and I could let my guard down. When I found myself withdrawing from high level conversations where I could flaunt my strengths and professional leverage, I knew that I valued a piece of mind and direct student work over office politics, clout, and titles.

In relation to a toxic environment, I would now say "no" to a company or organization that is not diverse and doesn't have the evidence to prove that they are fostering an inclusive workplace. Going from a PWI where I received my undergrad then to an HBCU where I received my graduate degrees, I have experienced the difference in my confidence and my emotional health. My feelings were confirmed where I left one job at PWI to another job at a HBCU. I found myself as a person and black scholar/scientist when I was at a HBCU and as black female leader when I worked for one.

Most people think that HBCUs are racially monolithic. That's further from the truth. They are greatly diverse in race, ethnicity, backgrounds and cultures. I felt comfortable being all of myself. I could easily switch from research to pop culture from Cardi B to the Clark Sisters and from sci-fi to Shea Moisture. It takes too much energy to pretend to be someone else or to hide pieces of you, especially if you must do it for 40 hours a week. Make sure you are some place where you can develop and evolve, and you feel like you are in a safe space. Even if you are not a minority, you should seek employers in which cultivate a diverse and inclusive environment as they will be more conducive to personal and professional growth.

Where I am in my personal and professional journey is that I value a peace of mind over money. I would rather take less money to have a productive and prosperous work experience. This doesn't mean I'm looking for perfection and "kumbaya" at every moment. I am looking for a practical, respectful, and inspirational atmosphere in which I enjoy coming to work every day. These are my list of values and expectations that I deem critical. Everyone has different needs. You have to be diligent in consistently reflecting on your values, your purpose, and your needs so that you can identify your non-negotiables.

Thou shalt maximize every opportunity.

I have heard many people say that they not doing more than what's on their job description. They precisely say, "they don't pay me enough to do all that." Going with this logic, you may be protecting yourself from being used by your employer. Yes, you don't want to be overworked and misused. But, if you flip your perspective, this doesn't have always be true. What if you were the one taking advantage of your employer and not the other way around? What if you were using them to find something better? That's exactly what I do in any position that I have. I learn and do as much as I can despite how I feel about the job itself or the boss that I work for. Any opportunity that allows me to network, learn something new, sharpen my skills or flex an unknown talent, I accept.

Dr. Erin Wheeler

My first position mainly involved me coaching students and working on resources for faculty. However, I knew what skills I needed to gain, and my boss had an intuition that I could do more than what my resume entailed. I worked on our departmental grants that provided opportunities to network with other leaders of departments and colleges. I ultimately took the lead on coordinating multi-unit and multi-institutional grants. This experience became a cornerstone of my career in higher education and my work with non-profits. Besides grant-writing, I leverage my experience in programming from my time in church and in student organizations to re-tool our tutor training and evaluation. I made the trainings more engaging and improved our recruitment efforts to encourage minority students to become tutors. I used my understanding of popular culture, and my age proximity to students to re-vamp the marketing and branding of our learning center. Even though I hated social media, I started the department's Twitter and Facebook account. In order to attract more students to become followers, I created events to engage with students and introduce our services in a positive light. More than 100 students attended the first event and 800 students attended the most recent event nearly six years later. And because of the initial success of our marketing efforts, I had an opportunity to help select and manage a Marketing & Communications intern. Later, I helped to select and collaborate with our department's first Marketing & Communications Coordinator. In addition to these projects I also served on several campus-wide committees that provided key experience in diversity, retention, and student engagement. All of this enhanced my resume and helped me to be recruited in a high-level position without many years of experience.

As an Assistant Provost, I had to take on different roles both out of a need to accelerate the progress of my direct work, but also because I was required to do so from leadership. While I had a separate staff to supervise, I was also a part of Academic Affairs, so I had to assist my colleagues in duties of the office. Because my previous employer was so big, I didn't have any opportunity to work in Academic Affairs. I really didn't even feel qualified to weigh in on anything, but I did not have that option because the work was so overwhelming, I had to jump in and help.

I found myself editing catalogs, conducting faculty meetings, re-vamping policies and procedures and writing accreditation reports.

Although I did not initially sign-up for any of that, I was grateful to have a chance to be front and center of operations in a higher education institution. If that wasn't enough, I was asked to temporarily lead enrollment management while a permanent leader was chosen, and organizational changes were made. I had some admissions experience (as an undergraduate) but no experience in leading financial aid or registrars' offices. It was trial by fire, but I love challenges. I took advantage of this leadership position make sure that students had a seamless transition from admissions to their second year to improve the success rates for students. It worked. We made big changes to orientation, New Student Week, and First-year Experience. That was the best year of my tenure. It was refreshing to have my ideas implemented from beginning to end and to work collaboratively (without a lot of BS) with my colleagues across campus. All those bonus experiences added a lot of stress and work to my plate, but it was worth it. I deepened my knowledge of higher education administration and operations without switching jobs.

Your first position may be "wack" (yes, that word choice shows my age.) and not your dream job. However, if you just do the bare minimum to earn your check, you are wasting your time. You need to learn as much as you can because you never know what experience you need down the line. Not only that, mastering skills and tasks outside your position can provide you insurance when it comes time for layoffs. You can increase your value by not doing the minimum. Now, let me be clear. This is not about working yourself to death. You need to be strategic in what tasks you take on in relation to your career trajectory.

Thou shalt build your own table.

In the previous commandment, I shared that learning and mastering roles and responsibilities outside of your job description can help shield you from layoffs. Remember, there are no guarantees in the workforce. You can absolutely lose your job at any time. It doesn't matter how long you've been on the job, what you've done for the organization, or your title. You are expendable. You have to be comfortable with that idea. It doesn't mean that you should always be paranoid, but you should always have a plan if a job goes away. Just look at the pandemic. Most industries that were solid and historically could weather any storm took a hit. Who knew that restaurants, bars and hotels would collapse? Anything can happen.

Take me for example. I did go above and beyond in my role as Assistant Provost. But that didn't stop a new President from coming in a cleaning house regardless of our previous work. After two and half years of hard work, my job ended. And, I was out of a job for nearly two more years after that. But don't cry for me, Argentina. I still made money. Was it six figures? No. Did it help me live my best life while not being on the clock for anyone? Yes! I continued to work on my hustle that I have had going for 10 years as well as initiate a new stream of income.

I've always been exposed to entrepreneurship. It's maybe not the ideal image of the businessmen you've seen on TV. Nope, my role models were my grandparents, my dad, and my uncle. They had some jobs here and there as I was growing up. But, for the most part they all had businesses and side hustles. My grandma ran a small restaurant and bar for our community. My grandfather owned rental property and delivered dirt and gravel to construction projects. My dad had his own auto shop business. He also took over my grandfather's rental properties. Once he retired from his job as school bus driver, he decided to be like my grandma and open a catering business serving lunches. Their entrepreneurial endeavors gave them the flexibility to focus on our family – me. I'm only joking a little. I was the baby of our family and enjoyed the spoils of people who were available for my demanding academic and social life.

Their hustle mentality rubbed off on me. It aligned with my list of negotiables, working for myself gave me what I genuinely wanted in my career: freedom to design my life and an outlet to be creative and innovative. I decided to focus on my business ideas after I completed my PhD. I knew that I had to have a business that I felt passionate about. If I don't care about it I am not going to work for it. Also, I did not want it to be all about the money and I wanted to build something that was on brand for me. So, I decided to open a college coaching business to serve my community and surrounding areas. I would offer some tutoring, but I really wanted to create a FOMO (fear of missing out) on getting services to help you prepare for college. My main offer was ACT Prep. I used this familiar request to create the conversation about what happens after getting admitted. My prices were not extremely high as I wanted to attract middle to low-income customers. I didn't make enough to quit my full-time job. But it was enough to close the gaps in my budget and add some relief to my strained finances. In addition, I created a non-profit to provide college prep summer camps for my hometown. When I moved to Kentucky, I couldn't continue to offer direct service, but I did work on re-branding and creating on online platform to enhance and expand coaching. However, once I came back home after I got laid off, I continued like I hadn't left. The income I generated help to sustain me during my two-year hiatus. In addition to my coaching business, I also created a consulting business in which I assisted higher education institutions improve their student support programs to increase the number of students completing college. My contracts were a major contributor of my income and allowed me to take my time entering back into the 9 to 5 world. During my time of formal unemployment, I also wrote my first book which used the money from sales to cover my expenses.

I have strategy that will allow me to grow my businesses alongside my career. My personal needs and desires fuel my passion for entrepreneurial endeavors. However, the way the world works now, you have to have multiple streams of income just have a basic life. You have to have a plan in order to proof your life against the dynamic workforce. You must have a way to monetize your talents and skills as a way to support yourself during a layoff. You should or in my opinion, you must, find a hustle or a side gig that will allow you to lessen the financial repercussions of not having a job. Now if want to put in extra energy to turn your hustle into a business that is another thing.

The whole idea of this career commandment is not just about creating opportunities for extra income. Creating your own opportunities can help you gain the experience you need to propel your career forward. You don't have to work for anyone to prove your value or define your livelihood. You can definitely do this on your own. In an award acceptance speech, billionaire playwright and movie producer, Tyler Perry, described his journey to success. He remarked on his constant rejection by Hollywood as he was trying to gain a seat at the table with power players and decision makers. Once he stopped trying to get their acceptance, he decided to build his own table instead of competing for a seat at someone else's. His words were validated my own feelings and strategies.

As you can recall in my story, I said that the ceiling was too low at my first job. After numerous rejections from my many job applications, I decided to get comfortable in the position even though I was unhappy. However, I began to shift my energy to creating an opportunity that allowed me to flex my leadership skills, implement my ideas, progress towards designing the life that I wanted. I began to focus on my college coaching company as well as creating my non-profit. Besides the experience I gained from each of these endeavors, the additional lines on my resume gave me depth and confidence-building talking points in my interview. Starting something on your own illustrates important skills such as leadership, initiative, critical thinking, and resilience. The outlets I created for myself also helped me to build my network, gain additional perspectives in education, and help more students. In both of my job transitions, it was my outside work that gave me the competitive edge I need to secure the job.

My years as an entrepreneur made me a good fit to become the Chief Executive Officer of a non-profit almost more than my years as a professional. As a "solo-prenurer," I was the innovation officer, the finance officer, the program manager, and the coach. I had already mastered multi-tasking and project management without constant oversight. I know without a shadow of a doubt that if I had not had the willpower to be consistent with my side hustles and business that I would not have been in a good place professionally or financially. I used to think this was uncommon. However, there are many professionals who are creating opportunities for themselves to advance their life and the career.

And if you have any doubt that employer's frown upon you doing things outside of your 9 to 5, dismiss that feeling. I felt that way. I was scared to admit that I was building something great in my personal time.

However, the more I read job descriptions the more I am sure that companies value the skills that entrepreneurs have. It is a different version of leadership. Some even say they are seeking candidates with an entrepreneurial spirit. They know that this person can take an unformed idea and turn it in to something great. Companies can't survive without innovation and evolution. They need their employees to help lead new endeavors just like a business owner grows a company. In fact, a lot of the companies you know now started inside larger companies as a simple project.

If you find yourself frustrated at the lack of job opportunities or you find yourself angry about the lack of resources and upward mobility at your current job, you should definitely devise a way to create your own lane to success. Build your own table and let others come and sit with you.

Thou shalt invest in yourself.

Like building your own table you need to also invest your growth. Degrees have a shelf life. Our world is changing so much that it is impossible to learn everything you need in four years. Even advanced degrees only serve as a foundation or launching pad for your career. You must be committed to lifelong learning if you want to successfully advance your career. While your employer may offer professional development opportunities, it also is important to learn to invest in yourself.

Being employed by a major university in an underfunded unit during major budget cuts sucks. There were often conferences to which I wanted to submit a proposal to become a presenter. My unit only had enough money to send two people to one conference per year. Any of my requests to any conferences that were not directly connected to our strategic plan or work were denied. I understood why, but it sucked. On my salary and with my bills, I could not really afford to pay myself. So, I had to think creatively to get the resources I need to grow professionally. What little professional development funding I was allotted went to books and webinars, which cost half of conference registration. I also evaluated my finances to see where I could save money to put towards my own professional development opportunities. I turned down fun travel in efforts to put more money towards personal conference travel. Sometimes I managed to combine personal and professional trips as a 2 for 1 deal. I presented with my sister and best friend in Hawaii at an American Counseling Association Conference. This sacrifice allowed me to diversify my resume while building my rapport in my field. That trip would have been immediately denied by my employer.

Another instance where the investment in myself paid off was when I was accepted into a start-up program for educators. The cost of the program wasn't exorbitant, but it took me a minute to save for it. It was definitely worth the effort. I learned so much about design thinking and growing a start-up. Five years later, the organization that hosted the program also played an integral role in helping shape the early years of the non-profit I currently work for. We are even housed in their co-working space. It eased the transition for me, as I recognized all the principles I learned in my program in the structure of the organization. It was a full circle moment for me, and it solidified the notion that effort and sacrifice always pay off no matter when you receive the return. There are so many professionals who are sharing their expertise through books, podcasts, courses, programs, and individual training sessions. There are so many affordable ways to learn new skills and grow as a professional. You just have to be intentional (there's that word again) and strategic to make things happen for yourself.

Besides resources to learn new things, you also need people to help you navigate your career. Investing in a career coach is one of the best things I've ever done. It might seem counterintuitive to spend a significant amount of money right after you've been laid off, but I knew that I needed someone to help me figure out my next move. I had become disenchanted with higher education as a whole. I really wanted to change my career path, but nothing interested me. I was so disappointed about my career outlook I was disengaged from the whole search process. My coach helped me through it all. I couldn't talk to my parents or friends about what I was feeling. He understood exactly the headspace I was in and helped me gain clarity. We worked on re-defining my values and non-negotiables. I discovered career options that still satisfied my need to remain connected to higher education but also addressed my personal career preferences. He helped me to optimize my LinkedIn page, refine my personal pitch, and improve my interview techniques. I honestly believed his services placed in me in the right position to be recruited for my current job—they found me on LinkedIn. And of course, I mentioned that I worked with another career coach who helped me to negotiate my salary. These two investments were pivotal to my success in my most recent job transition.

 As I am writing, I am taking a course on launching my productivity coaching business. I had been baulking at the price of so many similar courses. When, I found one that spoke directly to me and my needs, the shock of the price went away. It's one of the most expensive resources I've been investing in, but I've learned a lot so far. Soon, I'll invest in a certification program that will enhance my education leadership experience. Investing in yourself doesn't have to always mean paying a ton of money.

Investing your time, attention and effort to completing a helpful book or a podcast is just as important.

The workforce is extremely competitive. Your employer may not always be willing to foot the bill to help your grow professionally. You have to be willing to take on this task yourself. Life-long learning is essential to advancing your career.

Thou shalt network.

I hate the N-word, and by that, I mean "Network." I am really an introvert. I don't like small talk. I'm always trying not to be awkwardly silent and eerily shy. Conferences drain me. Emailing strangers make me anxious. Networking is scary for me. No matter if its face to face or virtually. However, networking is the key to navigating your career. Most jobs are not posted at all. And most jobs that are posted are just for show as they have already hand-picked the candidates and probably made an offer as the time of the posting. When you are a job seeker, it can seem quite messed up. But, if you step into the shoes of the employer, you can understand the logic albeit unfair.

As a person who has had to had to hire employees, I have recruited for positions in various ways. Some job openings I posted and casted a wide net for candidates. Some positions I have tailored to fit someone specifically. Other times, I have only posted and circulated to select groups to get the best recommendations. It just depends on the circumstances. Validating potential employees can be tiresome, and we want to just cut through the boring interviews and the monotonous steps and hire from our immediate networks. And that's usually what happens. If someone I trust sends me a person for a position, I am going to give that person preference. Maybe I'll give them an informal interview before the process starts or I'll fast track them to the final round. Most of the jobs I've gotten have been through knowing someone. Yet, on this last go round of job searches, I realized that I still have a way to go on developing my networking skills.

In applying for senior leadership positions at higher education institutions, I learned that I didn't have enough people in my network who were college Presidents, Vice-Presidents, or others who had influence over high profiled search and who could vouch for me. In fact, I had a search firm advise me that knowing either someone in a decision-making position or a search committee member increases your chances of selection. I knew she was right. I was striking out left and right on applications where I didn't know anyone. Even tracing back to see who was chosen for the position, I found out that, most times, I was more qualified than choice candidate. Putting on my private investigator and research hat, I immediately found connections between the choice candidate and the decision makers. Having someone vouch for your talent and provide you with an inside advantage is on par with being fully qualified for the job.

Now I have fully admitted that networking isn't my thing. I don't feel comfortable giving advice on this matter except to hone your networking skills. I'm still reading books and attending workshops to improve my networking skills as an introvert. But what I can offer you is that networking is not always about knowing a lot of people. It is about establishing and sustaining meaningful mutual beneficial relationships with others. One book that helped me to understand this is the classic book, *How to Win Friends and Influence People*. My career coach recommended it so I could learn how to authentically connect with new people in ways that were natural and easy.

Another piece of advice I've learned through observation is to not be one of those people who thirst after people with important titles. You never know who people know so be careful with just aiming for power-players. My personal approach which was validated by networking best practices is to make sure you treat the gatekeepers right. Many may overlook, secretaries, assistants, janitors, etc., but those are the ones who have the ear of the influencers and decision makers. They probably handle the application pools, set interviews, and schedule phone calls. This means anyone you know can be an asset. It also means you always need to present your best self and complete any task with excellence. Your work and your attitude will always proceed you and can impact whether your name is spoken in the circles of influence. People are not going to advocate on your behalf if they can't trust you and your work.

As you've entered the job market, I know you understand the frustration of completing a ton of applications only to get a handful of interviews. It's the worst part of job searching. However, I urge you, however, to do something a little counter intuitive. Spend more time making connections with the people in industries and companies you want to work for. This means attending events where they'll be present, connecting with them on LinkedIn, and requesting a short phone conversation to introduce yourself and learn more. You should also spend time researching companies, its leaders, and its employees. Taking a step back from desperately completing random applications gave me the peace and clarity I needed during my extended time of unemployment. Re-engaging with my sorority and participating in community events helped me to connect with people who could help me with potential job leads. Conducting informational interviews with people who took an alternative path in higher education provided me with insight and motivation to wait for the right opportunity. And, once I researched the organizations that had positions that I wanted to apply to, I learned enough not to waste my time applying.

In today's job market, networking is crucial. Even with companies doing more to improve diversity and move away from clique-ish hiring practices, there is still a need to get head of the application process and influence decision makers yourself.

Thou shalt lead & influence.

If you are looking to increase your salary, improving your leadership skills is a way to go. You don't have to have the title to be a leader. You don't even have to have people to supervise. You just need to be able to proactively solve problems, motivate others, and help your team move productively towards a common goal. There are all different kinds of leaders, you just have to tap into yours.

I am not the stand in front of people and give a rousing speech type of leader. I am the one who sits quietly in the cut until I have something substantive to say. I am the one who stealthily resolves tension amongst my peers by finding a compromise. I am the one who asks a question at the end of the meeting to help us determine next steps and not waste any more time in meetings. I am the person who can manage a project from idea to execution. That's my leadership style. It's not boisterous nor overbearing. Over the years, I realized that this was my magic ticket. I've now learned to articulate my leadership style in my interviews and cover letters more thoroughly.

Just as I discussed in the "Build Your Own Table" commandment, employers value individuals who can be leaders and can be managed with minimal oversight. They not only value it, they pay your more for it. It's rare occurrence to get paid the big bucks and not have some sort of leadership or management responsibility. You need to constantly be a scholar of leadership by reading books, listening to podcasts, or attending leadership trainings. Always aim to sharpen your communication, organization, and problem-solving skills. Strengthening your self-awareness is a must so that you can grow as a leader while remaining authentic.

Make no error in confusing titles with influence. To be an effective leader, you must know how to influence your peers as well as your superiors. Or else your title and your leadership ability will be called into question. Your success as a leader rests on the productivity and the collaboration of the people you are leading. You have to coax and inspire them to do what needs to be done to reach the common goal. You have to provide clarity in confusion and reassurance in instability. An influential leader calms fears, gives instructions, and resolves tension. To do this correctly, you must be empathetic and understanding to build individual relationships with others. You must learn how and why people think and behave so that you can foresee issues, tailor feedback, and make personal appeals to your team.

Being an influencer has been a talent of mine for a long time. Although I was a quiet person, I used my words very efficiently. My sister says that I always used to get over on our strict father, but she just always took "no" for answer. I did not. I knew why he was going to object to things. So, when it came to prom, I laid out a plan he couldn't refuse. I went both junior and senior years. My older sister, who is now 42, is still sour about this. I just thought this was something I was good at because I was the baby of the family. Turns out there are tons of books written to leaders to help expand their influence.

I had to influence a lot of people when I was Assistant Provost, especially if I need to change the culture surrounding supporting the needs of students. I had to win over faculty, my peers in other departments, and even my staff. I started with the loudest, most controversial, and unsatisfied people on campus. You know the ones who think they influence people by being negative and boisterous all the time. I introduced myself as soon as I arrived on campus. I invited them to coffee or lunch to chat. I asked them their opinions about their time at the university. I listened. And listened. And listened some more. I did this until everyone knew me. To my surprise, at the end of most conversations, they thanked me for listening to them. That's it. I had changed everyone's perception of me by just doing simple acts of kindness. I was no longer the young, new over-paid, admin who is just going to resign in six months. After I gave them my ear, they gave me their support. Before I made big changes, I would enlist the campus influencers to give me feedback so that I can plan to address the naysayers. This is how I was able to change policies, processes, and unproductive traditions without coming in like a bull in a china shop. I had sensed that those leaders who came before me did this repeatedly until the faculty and staff who had been there for years became resistant to change. I empathized with them when most just thought they were being jerks. They were just hurt from not having their ideas heard and not given the resources and support to do the work they were employed to do.

Influencing is not just for your colleagues and peers on your level, you should influence your superiors as well. I call this type of influence, "Managing Up." Managing up requires you to help your boss help you get your job done. Now there are some horrible bosses, but for the most part they are just overworked, unorganized, and exhausted. I am an independent worker; however, I thrive on feedback. What I hate most in this world is to put all my energy and time into a thing only to hear that it is wrong. I don't like do-overs. I like to make small corrections and not wide sweeping u-turns. So, I like to have access to my supervisor to get approval or questions answered so that I can remain productive. Like I understand that they may be in meetings all day and may take 24-36 hours to respond. But, if he/she is always too busy to keep our standing meetings or can't answer a simple text, I get aggravated. So, what I started doing is asking my bosses how they would like to communicate with me. I observe their patterns and habits. I try to understand the demands that's on them and try to help mitigate the pressure.

So, I'll give you three examples. I had three, technically six bosses during a two-year period. It was a circus. The first boss I had was phenomenal. Although she was super overworked and overwhelmed, she was incredibly efficient. In the weeks of me getting acclimated to my new position, I would email her several items every couple of days so she can address them in one swoop. She would clear off a nice chunk of time every other week so that we can catch up. That was all I needed. I'm not needy. I don't like hanging around the office or popping up to ask simple questions. Give me some undivided time regularly and I'll be happy. She left about two months after my arrival. I had to get reacquainted with another supervisor. This one was totally opposite. She could never gain her footing. She was never organized enough to keep up with emails. She would never put her foot down to stop the barrage of meetings that was always on her calendar. She was scattered and often stalled. I had to end up helping her with projects just to get one questioned answered or one document signed. But that time that I yielded to her caused me to be behind in my work. It was so bad that I had to circumvent her and report to her boss just to prevent my projects from stalling. Soon, my second boss made her exit. My third boss had inherited the same onslaught of work and constant fires. She and I eventually found our way. I realized that she never had a chance to eat. So, when I needed facetime with her, I ordered lunch or scheduled a dinner every Wednesday. I debriefed her on my area and followed up with an email reminder when needed. The other two bosses don't really count, but I did attempt to figure out their management preferences.

In all cases, I tried to be the one employee they didn't have to worry about. I made sure they knew clearly what my needs were and that they could count on me if they needed assistance. I also understood that it was my job to make them look good and be successful. My successes are theirs. Once you understand the gravity of a leadership position you can be a great servant-leader with a strong ability to manage-up. So, on your job, you should be working to establish meaningful working relationships so you can influence those around you to get things done and ultimately climb the leadership ladder.

Your career is such a big part of adulting post-grad. Working makes you question growing up and being responsible. And being a new professional while trying to figure yourself out is super stressful. You're trying to figure out the professional you *and* the personal you and determine how your two selves can get along. I wrote this chapter because it was the advice I wished I would have had early in my professional career. These things were learned the hard way. I don't recall any of my career preparation courses mentioning or explaining these things so explicitly. I don't want you to be completely shocked and dismayed about what you find out in the real professional world. Use the commandments to help you wisely navigate your career.

MAKING SENSE OF THE DOLLARS

Live Wiser

MAKING SENSE OF THE DOLLARS

As I am penning this chapter, I am sitting on my best friend's couch in California. We are four days removed from arriving back from driving in from Louisiana. I hate road trips, but it was the cheapest route to getting out of the house, having a pseudo-vacation, and spending time with my bestie in the middle of Covid-19. As we were binging on food and Marvel movies one night, I asked out loud something that's been rumbling around my head for years: "Whose insurance pays for the damage if you get caught up in a shootout or car chase if this movie really happened in the real world?" Yes, we adultified *Captain America: Winter Soldier*. At that moment, I realized that adulting just makes you question everything in life. Like nothing is as it seems anymore. Everything reminds you about bills, working, and taxes. Adulting just corrupts your imagination. And money seems to be the biggest offender.

The hardest parts of adulting, at least for me, center around money. Much of my anxiety revolves around finances. I think the lack of money combined with my need for perfection winds me up like those vintage wind-up toys. I hate checking my bank account and seeing so many deductions. I hate planning for big purchases. I hate doing taxes and thinking about insurance premiums. I hate confronting anything if I don't have the money to pay for it upfront. I hate asking for money, raising money, and I hate spending money. My wish one day is to not have to worry money at all and to have enough money in my bank accounts to live my life and to give to others.

My attitude towards money is one thing that I am focused on improving. I've come to learn that my negative perspective on finances inserts itself in every aspect of my life. It hinders my confidence as a Chief Executive Officer and entrepreneur to raise money, balance the budget, and make financial decisions. My neglect of caring for my own financial health puts my future at jeopardy. There's still a lot of growing I have to do in this area. But I still have a few pieces of advice to give from my financial journey.

Re-think wealth.

I used to think about being rich as having designer bags, luxury cars, and a nice home. However, that definition began to change as I matured. I think the change occurred once I bought my first home. I began to hate working a traditional job, and I began to put my priorities in order. As I emerged from my post-grad depression, I just remembered making the decision that I was happiest when I was doing something that I loved and was able to make sure my basic needs were met. I knew that that it was going to take discipline and clear focus to streamline my life and reduce my overall cost of living so that I didn't have to work full-time for someone else just to afford my life. I just hated spending so much time at work (that I wasn't overly fond of) just to afford a life I never had a chance to enjoy because I was at work and always exhausted. At the end of the day, I just wanted to be financially secure. I don't want to worry about money. If there is an emergency, I want to be able to handle it. If there is something that I must purchase, I want to be able to do it and not think for more than five seconds if the decision will land me on the streets. I know it's extreme. But that's the way my mind works. I told you. I'm in recovery for my financial anxiety. Turns out, my thinking is aligned with the definition of wealth. Being rich means you have a lot of money to cover a lot of expenses. Being wealthy means you don't have to worry about money. Wealth is best explained by time. How long can you go without working before you become at risk to lose your quality of life? Wealthy individuals have enough assets and very little liabilities that allows for a life in which they don't have to actively work—they can live off of their passive income.

In understanding this concept, I begin to analyze my life and make different financial goals that were totally opposite of my undergraduate dreams. For example, I decided to drive my 2009 Toyota Yaris for as long as I could or until I had a secondary source of income that would cover a new car note. I wanted to decrease the amount of bills I was responsible for and I wanted to put my extra money towards investments that increase their value over time. I also knew I had to be fiscally responsible so that my tiny, stagnant salary would go further. This meant I couldn't go on all the trips with the girls, that I couldn't do happy hours a few days a week plus brunch, and that I couldn't just go shopping when I wanted.

I also am on my eighth year of cutting the cord. I got rid of cable and subscribed to streaming services. I switched from a high price cell phone carrier to a pre-paid one. Yes, I was embarrassed when I first made these decisions because I was afraid to look like I was struggling. However, I quickly snapped out of that craziness when I pulled up to the gas station at the edge of campus and saw the President who made more than a quarter million per year drive up in a 10-year-old Honda CRV. At that moment, I realized I should make no apologies for securing my future.

Once I had this epiphany, I began to study the decisions of the wealthy. I learned that much of the glitz and glamour we see on TV is just for show and is characteristic of people who obsess about being rich. Look at the Bill Gates and Mark Zuckerburgs of the world. They are worth billions of dollars and still dress in old Old Navy clothes and drive a Prius to work every day. Oprah doesn't eat out and brings her lunch to work every day in plastic containers.

Mike Epps shared a story that further elucidates Oprah's fiscal conservatism. He recounted when he and Oprah were in a screen test which called for money to be thrown on the ground. He reached in his pocket and pulled out $20 of his own money to make the scene feel more realistic. At the end of the scene, someone whispered to him that he may want to pick up his money before Oprah takes it. He couldn't believe that one of the richest women on the earth would pick up a small bill off the ground. She gleefully confirmed what the others warned him about, and he indeed put his money back in his pocket. This also brings to mind hearing the advice Jay-Z and 50 Cent share young rappers and new black celebrities. They both talk about their transition from being rich to developing a wealth mindset. They both got rid of the jewelry and cars and put more focus on art, properties, and investments. They both stopped buying into the notion of looking like a million dollars to actually being worth a billion.

I am far from where I want to be, but I know that building wealth takes time. I am proud that I am taking small but necessary steps to be financially secure. I am at a place where I want to be a little more aggressive with reaching my goals because it feels like turning 50 is peering around the corner at me. I know what you are thinking because I thought the same thing. "Oh, I'm young, 45 is nearly two decades away." Life comes at you fast, and you will be staring at a half-century in the face. (By the way, I just turned 35 while finishing up this book).

Prepare like the future is tomorrow.

Although my parents couldn't serve as good career role models, they are good models for retirement. They retired from working relatively early and in good health. They retired while I was on my extended time of unemployment, so we were all at home just being footloose and fancy free. I watched them for years getting prepared for this time of their life. They were able to pay for their house in full by the time I graduated from high school when they were in their early 40's. They worked out their plans to pay down certain debt or complete certain big purchases for the house. They reduced where they could. They chose to buy certain vehicles that could be paid off close to retirement. I began to understand all the financial decisions they made throughout my life and why those decisions *now* make perfect sense to me.

While they made smart decisions when it came to long-term planning, I've seen the effects of not planning well. I've had family members or elders in the neighborhood who had to work until they were in really old and in poor health because they needed to make money to survive. Again, the definition of wealth is all about how much money must have to last you over a period of time. Unfortunately, for these individuals they didn't have much wealth, money, or assets to help sustain them over the latter years of their life. Yes, they did have social security, but that only covers a fraction of expenses, not to mention the increase in health care costs. Ultimately, they had to seek help from their children who also weren't prepared to support aging parents.

In studying economic mobility, which is the ability to change economic status in your lifetime, I've learned that not being able to handle financial emergencies, like taking care of a parent, keeps you from building wealth and climbing out of low-income situations. Not thinking about the future and living only in the present robs you of your financial security. You have to think strategically for yourself AND your family to safeguard yourself from financial ruins and protect your financial stability.

I know, one day, I'll be a multi-millionaire where I can put a considerable chunk of money into long-term investments, but for now I have to start small and start early. To build wealth, you either need a lot of time or a lot of money. For those of us who weren't born into trusts and have regular jobs, we have to take advantage of time to build wealth. Compound interest is the name of the game. Compound interest is where the money generated from the interest earned on your investment is re-invested to make even more money. The longer you invest, the better returns you have. The magic number seems to be $200. You need to save approximately $200 per month from the age of 25 to reach $500,000 by retirement at 65. You lose more than 50% by putting off saving for just a few years. So, when I locked on to the number of $200 per month, I realize that is totally possible for to do. It is challenging, but not impossible.

My biggest piece of advice to you is not to wait. You're expecting to live a long life, but you have to prepare for it. If you expect to actually have a significant number of years where you aren't obligated to work and have a high quality of life, you definitely need to be future minded. If you don't set the intent now and make an action plan for your financial future, you'll look up and you'll only have a few years left to retirement age and will not have a monthly income to sustain you. Go ahead and set up a retirement account. Take advantage of your employee match program or company stock options. Take advantage of investment tools that help you save and invest small amounts of money. Thinking about growing old can be scary but being unprepared is even scarier. That's why I present the next piece of advice.

Get a financial advisor.

Just like I would recommend a career coach to enhance your career journey, I would recommend a financial advisor. As a testament to my close circle, one of my friends connected me to his financial advisor. At first, I pushed back because I thought I didn't have enough money to be advised at 26. I'm so glad I agreed to meet with her. She introduced me to different types of investments that were more affordable if I took advantage of starting young. She exposed me to different types of life insurance policies that not only helped my family take care of arrangements after death but also provided me with benefits to withdraw cash if I needed to while I was living. We discussed long-term care options for myself as well as my parents. She made me become aware of things that I thought I had no chance of resolving until I encountered it like having to pay for in-home care or a facility for my aging parents or myself. She made sure my retirement contributions were up to par with my age and retirement goals. And she helped me to invest on a budget as well as challenged me to increase my investments over time. Honestly, I really wasn't thinking clearly about any of these big financial decisions until I met my advisor. She made things simple.

After, I began planning my financial future with her, I realized that there's so much that goes into being financially secure that the average person doesn't think about. When I counted up the cost of what I needed to take care of future Erin, I realized that I needed more than one source of income to comfortable right now and later on. This leads me to the next point.

Aim to achieve multiple streams of income.

I think my first time exposed to the seven streams of income was when Jay-Z was official deemed a billionaire and *Forbes* outlined how he amassed his assets. Once I did my research, I totally incorporated the idea into my financial plan. Seven streams of income stems from the idea that millionaires generate their total income from a variety of different ways. Of course, is first type of income is **earned income** meaning a job. This not a passive stream of income, as you must work for it. Most just rely on this type of income to live. Even if you're not aiming to be a millionaire, your job is barely enough to provide for your basic needs, which I why there is a need for alternate income. The second type of income stream is also not passive: **profit income**. Profit income is where you sell products or services over cost and benefit from the money you earn. This is where a side hustle or business applies. The third stream of income is **interest income** in which you earn money from interest generated from lending money to banks through saving accounts or government bonds.

Likewise, dividend *income* comes through investing in companies through stocks. When a company does well, it splits the profit among shareholders. This payment is known as a dividend. Rental income is the money made from renting any type of property and *capital gains* comes from selling something that has appreciated in value. For example, if you purchase a piece of artwork or a house for $250k and you are able to sell it for $400k, you would generate $150k in income. And lastly, *royalty income* is generated from letting others use any products, ideas, or services you've created. This is like authors earning money for book sales or singers getting paid for album sales.

There are pros and cons to each of the streams of income, and it'll take time to generate each stream. Think about how you can achieve some of these streams with the talents, interests, and resources you have over the long-term. The additional streams of income connect back to the career commandment of protecting yourself from layoffs and downturns. Having something in your back pocket can help you get through rough financial times. As you can recall, I mentioned that I was able to make money through my businesses and the royalties from my book. I didn't mention that I also had a rental property (my first home), and stocks that I sold to get by during unemployment. While it wasn't the same as having a full-time income, I was able to survive and take my time finding the right opportunity.

Appreciate Insurance.

Sometimes it's not about having a lot of money is also about protecting what you have. I used to think insurance was a scam. I would opt out of getting insurance on my rental cars. I would opt out of travel insurance. I didn't really want to read the fine print and understand my health insurance coverage. I don't know what turned me off about insurance, but I just didn't want to deal with it. Then, I felt the pain of being left out to dry with no insurance. That's nearly a literal interpretation. My home was hit with four feet of water in a rare flood in Baton Rouge. I had home insurance. I even agreed to upgrade and add in a Hurricane damage policy. Because the flood wasn't caused by a hurricane; my damages were not covered. To my surprise, I needed a flood policy. And a flood policy wasn't presented to me (at least I don't think it was) because I wasn't in a flood zone. I was numb. At the time, I was working out of state, and I wasn't living there. I had to receive the pictures to actually believe it was real. After having to borrow to remodel, I wished I would have had insurance because I am paying ten times more in loan repayments than in insurance premiums.

I am now a champion for insurance even though I still feel like it's a sucky concept. You feel like it's a waste of money because you aren't seeing the immediate benefit and you're paying for something that is a probability. It's a catch twenty-two. It's great when you don't have to make a claim but you're happy that you have resources when a crisis happens. Yes, there's a lot of fine print to read and it seems like they are trying to hit you with the okey doke. It's a wise financial move to protect your investments, no matter if it's your car, your home, your trip, or your health. Insurance is a financial tool to protect you. Insurance is not something you skimp on. Do your homework, read the fine print, and negotiate the best terms and price. And, speaking of doing your homework, you should analyze your financial literacy. See next point.

Continue to improve your financial literacy.

Although I have anxiety about finances, I do find security in learning more about money. One thing that the ultrawealthy have, besides advisors, is a wealth of knowledge. Yes, we received the basics of budgeting in our freshman seminar. We were told to stay away from credit cards and to make sure we pay our student loans. However, unless you are a business and finance major, you have a lot to learn about money. Learning about money should not just be about keeping the financial status quo, but it should be a means to wealth and financial empowerment. There are so many outlets to learn about wealth building strategies and keep up with the latest financial tips. The resources are plenty, but the hardest part is actually taking advantage of them. Life gets busy and the last thing you want to hear is about money when you are too pre-occupied with making it. It is a struggle for me. However, I try to work in audiobooks, podcasts, seminars into my daily life. You can even make sure you follow reputable influencers on social media. Just being exposed to simple tips can help enhance your financial planning and help you make better decisions which ultimately leads to greater wealth.

Another benefit to expanding your financial knowledge is that it helps you to shed inherited negative attitudes about money. Our families shape how we see and feel about money. Our financial perspective good or bad comes from what we have observed and how we lived as kids. For example, my parents did not buy into the notion of name brands. They valued quality but not names. I didn't have the latest shoes or labels, but we didn't shop at the Goodwill either. Of course, this played a major role in my confidence when I was a teen. Thank God my school district voted to have uniforms when I was in high school. At least I could splurge on shoes, because they didn't have to pay for real clothes. So, once I got some coins of my own, I began to fixate on what I couldn't have as a teen luxury name-brand purses, bags, shoes, and clothes. My eye always goes towards the most expensive item anywhere. My buying decisions, though, would be based what my parents would think. It takes me a long time to pull the trigger on purchases, big or small. I hear my mom's voice in the back of my mind calculating the costs and if the off-brand would be better. My dad, on the other hand, will not feel guilty about buying anything he wants. You can actually see this internal tug-of-war if you ever catch me in a store. I'll pick up items on one aisle, and then, you'll see me circle around to put things back. Then you may even see me pick up those same items I put back a few minutes later.

Our inherited views on money affect more than spending habits. It affects how risky we are with money and how much value we place on money. Improving your financial literacy helps you to examine your own pre-conceived notions about finances. Distinguishing money facts from fiction allows you to make better financial decisions. Just as you inherited your sense of money, you will pass down your money habits to your children and those around you. Therefore, changing your perspective of money gives you the power to break generational cycles of poverty and build generational wealth.

Establish your priorities.

Just as your goals and your purpose are unique, so are your financial goals. Establish your priorities according to you and not by anyone else's standards. This is definitely where adulting is the hardest. It is not wise to envy's everyone's life from a financial standpoint. Why? One can easily fake being rich. You see the car, the house, and the clothes, but you can't see the bank and credit card statements or their quality of life behind closed doors. When you count others' money, you'll surely make a fool out of yourself, and trying to live like them is surely a mistake.

In the previous chapters, I discussed how I had to make hard financial choices because of my personal priorities. I couldn't keep up with my friends. They immediately started working after college while I was in graduate school. By the time I had my first professional job, they had had nearly three-year head start with full-time, salaried positions. In my 20's, it was a hard decision to say no to things outside of my budget, but now in my 30's, it is so much easier. But even outside of the budget decisions, you have to consider that everyone's' values are different, and therefore, your priorities maybe different.

This means that some financial decisions are subjective even if they go against conventional financial wisdom. For example, I devalued going to the salon in my transition to go natural, and although I liked going to the nail shop, I would rather spend that money elsewhere. By elsewhere, I mean spending money on organic food, decadent desserts, and eating at great restaurants. Therefore, someone else may look at my budget and say I need to cut back in the food area, but that's not a place where I want to sacrifice. It is my one splurge. It makes me happy (food does make me happy, but also the social aspect of eating together). Individual values can affect everyday purchases, housing and car choices, and savings strategies. You can glean tips from others, but your budget and financial plan must be based your needs and your goals. Don't let anyone question your decisions, especially when they are grounded in your values and in the sound advice of expert.

Once you outline your personal goals and priorities, you should determine the cost of achieving those goals. Besides time and energy, designing the life the way you want requires some amount of financial contribution. Therefore, your financial plan should reflect your purpose and your aspirations. I used to get sad when I thought about where my money went. I felt that I didn't have anything to show for it. But once I really took stock of my spending habits, my money went to things that were important to me. I give a lot to my church. My faith is my number one priority. I allocate a lot of money to my home, which is an asset, and is part of my financial plan to own real estate. Over the years, my extra coins have been going towards bootstrapping my business. I also invest a portion of what could be my play money into stocks, which also plays a part of my long-term financial goals. Although it's taken some time, I've grown comfortable with my financial decisions as I have celebrated the milestones in reaching my personal goals.

Staying true to yourself and your life plan is difficult, especially in the financial sense. It contributes to a lot of dilemmas as an adult. We have been taught that money and stature define us. It doesn't. But the expectation adds pressure to make decisions that will affect our relationship with money. You will encounter financial crises no matter how much money you have. Biggie rapped about having more money and more problems for a reason. So, don't just aim to get rich. Aim to be prepared, financially savvy, and financially secure so you can navigate and enjoy both your harvest seasons and your lean times.

LIVE WISER

Live Wiser

LIVE WISER

Wisdom is the principal thing; therefore, get wisdom: and with all thy getting get understanding. Proverbs 4:7

I wrote this book to provide my wisdom so that you can have a more accurate understanding of adulting after college. Wisdom is important part of my life and success. As the baby of a very conservative family, I spent a lot of time around adults and not around kids my own age. As a child, my father had the same experience and credited his success to hearing the homespun wisdom of elders in his community and family. My mother, whose mother died young, also had that experience when the older ladies in our community served as surrogate mothers. They both wanted to provide that same exposure for my sister and me. I always seemed mature for my age in all phases of my life. I credited it to listening and learning from adults around me. For me, I can be a little prudish (I quit caring what others had to say). I was slow to peer pressure and living the "YOLO" motto. I just never wanted to be a cautionary tale. I didn't see myself as different from anyone else, so if they made bad decisions and had negative outcomes, then I know if I made bad decisions, I would suffer the same fate. I didn't have to learn the hard way, which saved me from falling into the pitfalls in life. Not falling for the same life traps as others helped me to accelerate my success. Carefully observing and understanding the thoughts and actions of others helped me to control what I could of my future and choose differently. For me, it's like some telling you what's on the test before you took it, so you can study the right things to pass the test. They may have failed it, but now their liberal insight prevents you from making the same mistakes.

Live Wiser is a study guide to adulting. I did okay on my test. I didn't flunk, but I didn't get an "A" either. So, I've shared with you what's going to be on the test in Adulting 101. I want you to not make the same adulting mistakes as myself or my millions of my millennial peers (or you parents). I especially want to prevent you falling into or (help you get out of) post-grad depression because of a false idea of what life should be after college. This doesn't mean that you won't make mistakes. It means that you'll make new ones, and, hopefully, you'll combine my wisdom with your new wisdom, and help another wave of new college graduates to "adult" better.

This book is just one perspective of adulting after college. Truly living wiser means that you are constantly observing and learning from the life of others. Living wiser involves gathering as much foresight as possible so that are able to sustain progression towards the life you desire. Living wiser, however, does not require you to emulate the exact actions others. It entails extracting and synthesizing information from the actions and outcomes of others so that you can make better decisions. No one can rewind their own life to fix regrets. But we can see our past reflected in someone's present. I think it is a waste of my time and energy if I can't pay it forward and help someone else avoid the pain and embarrassment of the mistakes I've made. It's a waste of my life if I don't share with others how I did manage to get some things right. Some parts of adulting are too painful to re-open and share with others. I think that's why so many college graduates are entering life after college blindly. Those who have gone before us didn't really have the willpower to disclose how their life unfolded. I totally get it. This book was so hard to write. Dredging up some of the hardest moments of my life while trying to balance optimism and realism was a challenge. But it was a cathartic experience and I really wanted to help others like myself. As a minority, first-generation, low-income college graduate, I didn't have a lot of people who could help me in my college journey. I had even fewer people who could help me make sense of my life after college and who could understand exactly what I was feeling and experiencing in my life.

After reading this book, I hope you understand that you are not alone in experiencing the raw and rocky emotional transition into adulthood. I hope that I have armed you with enough information to fearlessly conquer your 20's and beyond. I sincerely mean this, please connect with me on social media. I would love to hear from you and flow your journey. I'll have my sunglasses ready for the moment that Grown-Up Glow-up emerges.

www.ingramcontent.com/pod-product-compliance
Lightning Source LLC
Chambersburg PA
CBHW021941290426
44108CB00012B/919